*Mallarmé,*
*or the Poet of Nothingness*

# Jean-Paul Sartre

## *Mallarmé,*
## *or the*
## *Poet of Nothingness*

Translated and Introduced by
**Ernest Sturm**

The Pennsylvania State University Press
University Park and London

This translation is based on the authoritative French edition established by Arlette Elkaïm-Sartre and published in 1986 under the title: *Mallarmé: La Lucidité et sa face d'ombre*. Editions Gallimard, "Collection Arcades," © 1986 Paris.

Library of Congress Cataloging-in-Publication Data

Sartre, Jean Paul, 1905–1980
Mallarmé, or, The poet of nothingness.

Bibliography: p.
1. Mallarmé, Stéphane, 1848–1898. 2. Poets,
French—19th century—Biography. 3. Psychoanalysis
and literature. 4. French literature—19th century—
History and criticism. I. Title. II. Title:
Mallarmé. III. Title: Poet of nothingness.
PQ2344.Z5S2713     1987     841'.8     86–43027
ISBN 0-271-00498-3

To Carl Lesnor, *vieux copain,*
without whom this would have been
the translation that might have been

# Contents

# Acknowledgments

I am indebted to Robert Gallimard, of Editions Gallimard, for authorizing the present translation; to Arlette Elkaïm-Sartre, who read the manuscript carefully; to André Schiffrin, Managing Director of Pantheon Books, for releasing his option rights; to the Georges Borchardt Agency, for attending to legal formalities; and to the late Simone de Beauvoir, for her gracious support.

My special thanks go to Michel Sicard, a distinguished Sartrian who first published this text in *Obliques* and pointed me to it; to FUKA, for coping with me; to Professor Norman Rudich, for his penetrating observations; to Donald McDonald, Acting Director of the Center for the Study of Democratic Institutions, and to Professor Donald Pearce, of the UCSB English Department, for their valuable suggestions; to Vaughn Boyle and Michael West, for a fine word-processing job; to Philip Winsor, Senior Editor of Penn State Press, a gentleman of the vintage variety.

# Introduction

*Nothing is but what is not.*
*—Shakespeare*

I

What made Jean-Paul Sartre, the philosopher of commitment, turn aside from his pressing *engagements* of the early Fifties and launch into a major theoretical analysis of a poet who seemed the very embodiment of detachment?[1] After all, in *What is Literature?* (1947),[2] Sartre had banished poets from his Republic of Committed Prose. Why, then, did he admit Mallarmé?

For one thing, both were convinced that Being was rooted in Nothingness—that alone would have sufficed to bring Mallarmé under Sartre's jurisdiction. But what especially intrigued Sartre was the way Mallarmé's unsettling negativity undermined the very substance of poetry: nature, society, the person of the poet himself. He once called Mallarmé "our greatest poet"[3]—a greatness enhanced by what Sartre perceived, paradoxically, as deficiencies redeemed by the poet's life "project."[4]

In *The Poet of Nothingness*, Sartre's intention is not to explicate Mallarmé's art—the reader should turn elsewhere for glosses—but to measure the often-morbid social, psychological, and literary features of Mallarmé's world and thereby to lay bare cultural patterns that gradually hardened into our own century's modernist ethos. The work is divided into four parts.[5] *The Atheist Heritage* (I) examines the politics of poetry by probing into the destiny of a literary generation that saw the failed Revolution of 1848 freeze the class struggle and impose on the bourgeoisie the unsavory task of consolidating its power. *The Chosen One: A Phantom Marriage* (II, 1) presents a cameo of Mallarmé in his private and professional life—a gloomy life—in the company of his self-effacing wife, his dutiful daughter, and his literary cohorts, all the while serving time as a teacher of English. A sentence from his own English textbook illustrating the use of the definite article epitomizes his existence: "Feather by feather, *the goose* is plucked."[6] *The Dead Hand of the Past* (II, 2) measures the poet as an impaired product of the societal forces that bore down on his life and which he struggles to convert into the "universalizing singularity"[7] of his artistic project. Freedom—its nature and possibilities—is contemplated in a case where the odds appear hopeless. The closing section (III) is Sartre's requiem for the poet, whose deconstruction of language, like Schönberg's dissolution of traditional tonality, foreshadowed those modernists who were to dominate aesthetics a half-century later.[8]

If, as Engels believed, history is "the ascent of man from the kingdom of necessity to the kingdom of freedom,"[9] the disappointed social expectations of the mid-nineteenth century clouded this honorable prospect with doubts, if not despair. The fall of the July Monarchy and the miscarriage of the Revolution of 1848 affected the entire intellectual order of the age. The prevailing mood became one of disbelief, disillusionment, and resignation. With the screen of royalty removed, it became clear that a small, parasitic ruling class was perpetuating, by every means at its disposal, economic and political domination over the newer, industrialized working masses. The "higher values"—science, religion, the arts—reflected this fact of bourgeois culture.[10]

After the emotional surge of a revolutionary experience, European man found himself at an impasse where, in Yeats's words, "the intellect no longer knows *Is* from the *Ought*, or *Knower* from the *Known*."[11] In a society shaped by material acquisitiveness and exploitation, the spiritual *telos* of European man no longer had a haven. God could no longer be identified as a universalizing principle: From the time of Kant, critical analytic reason—"that most potent of bourgeois weapons"[12]—had shifted the burden of creativity to Man. But the rule of Man had not succeeded in supplanting the rule of God. The bourgeoisie—formerly the class of progress speaking for Humanity in the name of Reason—now adjusted its definition of Reason to legitimate and anoint its own interests. In a parody of human aspirations, it sublimated its doctrines into ghostly essences. God's role as spiritual caretaker of the established order had become unmistakable. The consequence was an eruption of disbelief: "The old religion is radically dead," wrote Heine. "The majority of Frenchmen no longer want to hear any talk about this cadaver, and cover up their nose with a handkerchief whenever the question of the Church comes up."[13]

The effects on Western consciousness of this loss of faith, how it made itself felt on two generations of poets—from Baudelaire to Mallarmé—are limned in *The Poet of Nothingness*. The poets who flourish after the middle of the nineteenth century are unbelievers, though not without twinges of nostalgia for the reassuring symmetry of a God-ordered universe. They cannot reconcile themselves to the makeshift divinity who had been enlisted to sanctify the interests of the "bourgeois" social order; at the same time the concept of Nature, which had depended on God as its final cause, undergoes radical transformation. Once encountered as a great Chain of Being, as a creative power indwelling in the world, it had become just another dimension reflecting the control of man. Rather than offering the poet a privileged realm of erotic cathexis, nature now presents the unsightly scars of pragmatic bourgeois reason.[14] Mechanistic and indifferent, it had taken on the features of inert matter. "Nature," quips Sartre, had become "an infinite dance of dust particles."[15]

Henceforth poets could look neither to Heaven nor to Nature for meaning and renewal. Sartre conjectures that it was the poets' isolation from the working-class movement that more than anything else turned them into victims choked by their own class, whose values they despised but elected out of self-interest. Unable to make common cause with the disenfranchised, they project their grievances onto the metaphysical realm. Since history seemed to have exhausted its teleological potential, their revolt becomes cosmic instead of social, symbolic and imaginary instead of real. "The wrath of the poets was awesome," writes Sartre. "The most violent immediately proclaimed their hatred of Man, that impostor whose grievous fault consisted in not being the son of God."[16] They plunged into somber glee at the idea of mass destruction or decline:

> Man, heir of man and of his accrued evils
> With your dead planet and your vanished Gods,
> Fly away, vile dust . . .[17]

The previous generation of Romantic poets—Lamartine, Vigny, Hugo, Musset—had fared better. Even the few atheists among them never doubted the existence of Truth, Beauty, and Good. Baudelaire, who straddled both halves of the century, could still "[draw] on God to supply his intimate ecstasies while denying his existence."[18] Vigny remained persuaded that "poetic madness [was] sacred."[19] After mid-century, however, the poets "saw the Divine Idea run out of steam, the celestial lights go out, and Platonic Truth turn into Illusion. Before they even had a chance to comprehend this sleight-of-hand, they had lost everything: the principal subject of their poetic meditations, the guarantee of their genius, their position in society."[20]

The crisis of disbelief invaded the aesthetic realm. It was inevitable that the poets' aversion to practical reality should cast its shadow on the exercise of their art. Previously, a poem had been providentially inspired: "The poet was only the trumpet; God supplied the breath."[21] The post-Romantics, however, tended to view themselves as "a grotesque tin horn that echoes the discordant noises of Nature."[22] In this era of lost illusions, Nature was no longer revered as a principle of replenishment and growth; rather, it served to mirror the poets' self-estrangement. In 1852 Baudelaire wrote about the cruelty of the sun and sought to "punish" Nature by striking down a flower.[23] "For our Atheists-in-spite-of-Themselves," writes Sartre, "all that exists reflects back on the vain and absurd image of their being. In every pebble, in every rose, they perceive their own perfect incongruity. They begin to call this direct intuition of Being *ennui*."[24]

In a God-forsaken world where man stood estranged from nature and no longer felt in charge of his destiny, there was little room for rhapsody. Nor could the society which now ruled History and which made Proudhon declare that "he was carrying on a war against cannibals"[25] give comfort to these disillusioned souls. Yet as members of the *petite bourgeoisie*, they tended to reproduce its utilitarian goals by bowing to the demands of their families and their milieu, where the "iron cage"[26] of institutions awaited them. Their bitterness and anger were sublimated into poetry. To whom should this poetry be addressed? Surely not to the bourgeois public, which embodied the very values they hated. To whom then? Deep down, these post-Romantic spirits suspected that poetry had gone out of business and that few people really cared about what they had to say.

In a theater full of empty seats, poets became their own favorite audience. They established a quixotic elite, a forlorn knighthood with aristocratic and idealistic pretensions; huddled together in their sanitized ivory tower, they would "prove their superiority through denial, through their contempt for life and nature, through negativity."[27]

This transcendental ploy, however, was not successful. Sartre calls it "an act of negation emptied of content."[28] Yet they soberly rediscovered content once poverty came knocking at their door. Ironically, too, they unwittingly reproduced the work ethic in the aesthetic realm through an "inner-worldly asceticism" that is generally acknowledged as the rule-of-thumb characterization of the spirit of early capitalism. Afflicted by such contradictions, they enjoyed transposing the "social drama into a cosmic catastrophe":[29]

> A dead world, immense sea foam,
> A gulf of sterile shadows and spectral lights . . .[30]

"If they endeavored to bring about this fictitious and radical abolition of the Universe," says Sartre derisively, "it was to appease their rancor without compromising themselves. It seemed more comfortable and less dangerous to imagine the sun cooling off than to deal with the social order."[31] Such was the climate of poetry in the latter half of the century.

What distinguishes Mallarmé from his contemporaries? "Most of them," says Sartre, "won't see things through to the end; they give up midway, allowing themselves to trail off into apathy, transitory passions, or whimpering narcissism. Not one of them is capable of holding together, in a single overarching tension, the various and contradictory aspects of their situation and their options."[32] Mallarmé, who was plagued by impotence, exhausted by insomnia, and tormented by physical pain, became the nerve center of the crisis in post-Romantic "higher culture." "If someone could appear for whom the idea of poetry could become a mortal and self-inflicted illness, if an all-embracing lucid consciousness could, in one single act, hold all its nuances together . . . If all the errors were stacked to the limit, they would topple over and reveal the truth of man behind them." If someone doesn't step forward and volunteer to live them out, "these daydreams would testify to the asphyxiation of French thought in the nineteenth century or to the human condition itself."[33]

Rising above the cultural confines of his day, Mallarmé, in Hegelian world-historical fashion, heroically volunteered.

For Jean-Paul Sartre, man defines himself through his struggle as a conscious subject coming to grips with his reality. To tackle the intricacies of this struggle, Sartre, like so many searching intellectuals of his day, looked to Marxist and Freudian doctrine. In a candid passage, he suggests that his interest in Mallarmé was ancillary to a more basic concern in exploring a particular analytic method. "If we have chosen the case of the 'Obscure Sphinx of Tournon' [Mallarmé], it is because it seemed to provide us with the privileged opportunity to confront, in a concrete case, the psychoanalytic and Marxist methods of interpretation."[34] Needless to say, in his endeavor to appropriate both of these methods, Sartre puts their compatibility to the test.

Sartre implicitly grounds his analysis on the Marxist proposition that Art is a product of the division of labor, which at a certain stage of history results in the separation of material from intellectual work, bringing into existence a group of artists relatively divorced from the means of material production. During the period of history that Sartre is describing, we have seen that this "divorce" gives rise to a "pure" aristocracy of thought and sensitivity. The poet now imagines himself as belonging, by his unique gifts, to a classless spiritual caste that safely shelters him from mundane reality. His rage, savage condescension, and air of long-suffering endurance tend to be predicated on some psychological or intellectual metaphor for the principle of aristocratic ranking. To become noble, one's own nature must be denied through Absolute Art. By the middle of the century, this fanciful mythology is comparable to a "mild case of schizophrenia without actual delirium":[35]

Void son of the Void, of what do you complain?[36]

Detached from the human condition, the artist becomes a stranger inhabiting an alien universe:

I wandered alone on the Earth, and the Earth was bare;
Through the endless void, the denuded globe . . .
Sailed off . . .[37]

As the metaphysical sequel to their attitude of absolute negation, the poets discover universal Nothingness. Mallarmé will affix his personal stamp on the negative universal image that his fellow poets project on mankind. His verse, reflecting the neurosis of the *"objective spirit"* of society,[38] is a distillation of the cultural condition of his time.

From 1850 to the early twentieth century, from the post-Romantic generation to the last Symbolists, writing meant exile. To write was to engage in an activity external to life, to undergo depersonalization, to struggle with an occupational disease. The literary doctrines of the period, such as those advanced by Verlaine and Leconte de Lisle, represent pseudomasochistic prolongations of the experience felt by individuals baffled by the mechanisms of the world that confronts them. Verlaine dismisses "superb and sovereign Inspiration"[39] as fancy. Poetry is henceforth to be forged by "unheard-of effort, supreme struggle."[40] The poets' heroic self-exertion, glum self-discipline, and patterns of failure "constitute," says Sartre, "if not the ideology of the *petits bourgeois*—they never had any—then at least their ideological complex."[41] The divorce of poetry from reality did not withstand the mutilating effects of the Performance Principle that safeguards the system of operational ruling-class values.

Sartre endeavors to understand Mallarmé in the context of the history of the French bourgeoisie of the nineteenth century as depicted by Marxist accounts—an approach he would later amplify in his very large study of Flaubert, *The Idiot of the Family* (1971, 72). Yet he felt it indispensable to separate himself from those "formalist" interpreters of Marx whom he reproached for flattening out the aesthetic experience by conflating it with its social determinants. He agrees with the dialectical concept blocked out by Marx in his third *Thesis on Feuerbach:* "The materialist doctrine that men are products of circumstances and upbringing and that, therefore, changed men are products of other circumstances and changed upbringing, forgets that it is men who change circumstances and that the educator himself needs educating."[42]

Sartre's own method seeks to safeguard the poet's "bitter furies of complexity"[43] while at the same time remaining alert to the concrete historical forces shaping his world. Since this world is conditioned by personal as well as social variables, Sartre looks to psychoanalysis as a complementary interpretative tool, but one to be used with utmost care so as to prevent ideological collisions. Here as elsewhere, he is as wary of Freudian as he is of Marxist orthodoxy, for he feels that its functionalist, deterministic categories fetishize convention and clash with his ontology of freedom and choice. The issue pivots on the crucial question of method: How can a biographer recover the restless inner movements of a reflexive consciousness? How can he then follow the paths by which these movements climax in a work of art at a given stage of historical development? For Sartre, the different dimensions of human reality can only be grasped phenomenologically: "*the way* [*man*] *fits into the very heart* of human reality, *the extent to which he is affected by the world,* his *absolute distance* from concrete reality."[44] Psychoanalysis, Sartre contends, is impaired by positivist components incompatible with these central structures which connect a person to the Whole and which are at the core of Sartre's own theory of Being. It tends to mirror back the slick, mechanistic categories into which human social existence is locked. Magpieing from Heidegger, Sartre stresses the "ontic" bonds that link an individual to Being and which, in their totality, determine his way of *Being-in-the-World.*

In his wish to outbid Freudian metapsychology, Sartre puts his own syncretism to the test. Husserl's critique of empirical psychology and Heidegger's approach to social theory, where the Other is encountered in his *Dasein* with and in the world, are both visible in this endeavor to isolate Mallarmé's dissonant mode of perceiving reality.

It will be seen, moreover, that Mallarmé is perceived as a subject who consciously forged a unique artistic project which, in Lukács's words, overturned "the whole illusion-creating totality from 'within.' "[45] Arguing from a position that goes back to *Being and Nothingness,* in which the philosopher set out to undermine the notion of the unconscious by showing how it can be turned into an instrument of bad faith (like a lie without a liar), Sartre insists that Mallarmé's singular *poesis* grew out of a series of conscious choices exercised on the basis of prior conditions. Sartre does not minimize the immense weight of these conditions or the strenuous efforts required to overcome them.


## II

*The cradle rocks above an abyss.*[46]
—*Nabokov*


In a world where there are only societies based on exploitation, "everyone is lost since childhood."[47] To fathom the adult poet and his artistic project, Sartre looks back to Mallarmé's earliest years, for "we live our childhood as our *future.* It determines our gestures and roles in a future perspective."[48]

Bismarck's inspired remark that the purpose of life is to fill out forms seems to have been expressly designed for Mallarmé. In his brief autobiography, Mallarmé wrote that "ever since the Revolution both my maternal and paternal families made up an uninter-

rupted line of functionaries. . . . the career for which I was destined
from the cradle was in the Recorder's Office."[49]

> Frigid roses all destined to live
> Alike . . .[50]

Born into the fusty milieu of the civil service, where offspring were
conceived as family hostages, Mallarmé found himself in a world in
which "pledges" had already been given on his behalf.[51] A language, a future career, values—all these had been prepared for
him. He had been pledged by proxy: "The destiny of the newborn
child is so entirely prearranged that it is no longer clear whether a
birth or death is being commemorated. But so many bureaucratic
guardian angels were watching over this cradle that great expectations were in order. One day they will observe the emergence of a
fastidious little bug, nimble, fully formed, and ready to propagate
the species."[52]

In Sartrian words, an individual who enters a group realizes that
its former "totalization" has marked the limits for his own conduct.
Within this context, he carries on his own totalizing operation.[53]
His "truth" is anchored both within him and outside him, for he is
at once a reflexive consciousness and a social product.[54] Born into
a clan of *fonctionnaires* who attempted to hammer him, from infancy, into one of their own, Mallarmé strove desperately to forge
his own history against the tyranny of his milieu by turning its very
own instruments against it.

When he was five, his mother died. This was the dark event of his
young life which, more than any other, would color and shape his
future. In infancy, a child experiences the world through the eyes
of his mother: "He takes refuge *from everyone* in his mother's
gaze. . . . He exists because she looks upon him; his truth is in her.
What is more, she lends him her eyes."[55] For the phenomenolo-
gist, visual perception is crucial; it is the nature of the Gaze that will
reveal that nature of Mallarmé's Oedipal bond.

With the death of Mallarmé's mother, "the Gaze is extinguished."[56] Things take on an imperceptible distance, acquiring the
coloration of "elusive objects which [are] lacking something":[57]

"Was it a dream I loved?"[58] Mallarmé loses his mother just as he begins to distance himself from her so that he might perceive the world autonomously. In her presence, things once had an irresistible shimmer; but now his unweaned, yearning eyes see only a hollow shell whose contents he perpetually tries to restore in a desperate need to bring the dead back to life. Instead of conjuring up Being, however, the bereaved child "swerved in naught,"[59] scraping among "the ashes and cinders which remain after the flames of a dream have died out."[60]

Between the vision of childhood and that of adult perception, there is an ontological rift. The child he once was and who touched, smelled, and tasted the world, who looked on it with innocent awe, haunts the adult poet as a bygone dream.

> . . . raindrop and diamond, transparent gaze
> Resting on these never-wilting flowers.[61]

Mallarmé must constantly link this dream to his mother's loss. Because maternal presence and richness of perception stand in mutual relation, he is condemned endlessly to conjure up the maternal shadow. This ghostly round of absence and presence confines him to a state of limbo where people and things are pure potentiality, empty, a source of regret. What he lacks cannot be found by searching for it. Beside himself with despair, the poet comes to the realization that conventional language cannot convey his plight—whereupon he invents a verbal sleight-of-hand to convert the fleeting richness of Non-being into Being and the poverty of Being into Nothingness.

Sartre, like Freud, dwells on the decisiveness of childhood experience. Just as Jean Genet became a thief because he was wrongfully accused of stealing when he was ten, Mallarmé became the Poet of Nothingness because his mother had the bad grace to die at an inopportune moment of his development. A fortuitous event would define the nature of his freedom, his choices, his project. But this is only part of the story; the rest concerns the poet's efforts to break away from the blood ties, institutions, and class which made claims on him. Henceforth, there are only Mallarmé's awkward efforts to devise desperate strategies of survival to overcome his personal history. His struggles to go beyond himself are seen at different levels of integration and complexity in the evolution of his slender literary testament, whose "leaps of implication" were to change the face of modern poetry.

Sartre's equivocal position toward the literary figures he chose to write about is well known. With the exception of the "saintly" Genet, who refused to be shattered by the troubled fantasies that nourished his career as thief and writer, Sartre was ambivalent toward his biographical subjects. Baudelaire—the first of Sartre's portraits of major writers—was faulted not for having written a poetry of inner collapse but for having cultivated inner collapse (a judgment Sartre would subsequently moderate). Flaubert stirred in Sartre feelings of fascination and revulsion which were never satisfactorily resolved.[62] And Mallarmé? This "gentle and wretched poet," writes Sartre, "who went about his job without too much effort and suffered conveniently from the prevalent Mid-Century Malaise"[63] of *ennui*, also produced a poetic corpus of "revolutionary dimension." "Mallarmé was the first to raise the still timely question: 'Does anything like literature actually exist?' . . .* After him, there is no turning back. From the moment he decided to write so as to plunge the Word into an adventure from which there was no turning back, there has been no writer, however modest, who has not put the Word itself into question."[64] "After reading Mallarmé," declared Valéry, "everything else seemed cowardly and naive."[65]

What are the essential contours of this new *poesis*? In his famous *Lettre du Voyant* (1871), Arthur Rimbaud announced that conventional syntax and grammar had become obsolete and that to ex-

---

*To be sure, the question addresses itself not only to the *social* but also to the *private* function of literature as Value. In *Nausea*, the prewar Sartre had singled out writing as a privileged transcendental realm of personal praxis: I write, therefore I am. But already in 1953–54, when Sartre was working on a first draft of *The Words*, he sniffed at his own deep-rooted veneration of literature, denouncing it as a "neurotic" idealism he had cultivated since the age of nine. Yet he continued to write, a creature of habit—*nulla dies sine linea*—until brought to a halt by deteriorating blindness.

In 1975, in the course of a seminar, the psychoanalyst Jacques Lacan snapped: "The writing-cure? I don't believe in it!"

press the ineffable a new idiom was needed which "would resume everything—perfumes, sounds, colors."[66] Shortly thereafter, Rimbaud discarded his visions as fancies. During the next twenty years, the poetic enterprise "grows out of the stony rubbish"[67] of existence where language itself is conceived of as "a handful of dust."[68]

This brings European literature to an unprecedented pass. The language which summons an individual when he enters history and begins to utter the sounds of his culture becomes the broken murmurings of "an epoch troubled by the trembling of the veil of the temple."[69] With Mallarmé, language is relentlessly pursued by its own negation: "We utter words only 'to plunge them back into their own futility.' "[70] After Mallarmé, poetry becomes the formal embodiment of a verbal pathology: the poem that might have been, the poem that might be if the world could ever be made anew.

Mallarmé's poetry shuns inspiration from the concrete world. As spokesman for the realm of Nonexistence, the poet has no solution other than to break with established forms of discourse. Unable to establish complicity with the world or to experience objects in their solid, reassuring neutrality, he summons up images which, no sooner evoked, collapse back into non-being. Meaning springs from "the *absence* of certain objects," from "the negation of the word's status as a thing," from a "resonant disappearance."[71]

> I say, 'a flower!' and from beyond the oblivion to which my voice banishes any contour, musically there emerges, as something other than known calyxes, its very sweet idea— missing from all bouquets.
>
> [Je dis: 'une fleur!' et, hors de l'oubli où ma voix relègue aucun contour, en tant que quelque chose d'autre que les calices sus, musicalement se lève, idée même et suave, l'absente de tous bouquets.][72]

No *particular* plant can satisfy this generalized concept of flower. Poetry now seeks to abolish objects.

Beset by visions offended by reality, Mallarmé chafed under the insufficiencies of language as a way of voicing his fragile link to a world that had become no more than a pretext for poetry writing. In 1864, while composing *Hérodiade,* he announced the immodest nature of his enterprise: "I am inventing a language." Established discourse is henceforth the foe. "In the face of that Nothingness which is the Truth,"[73] the poet becomes a lexical exile. His "native illumination"[74] that words are the sole manufacturers of meaning explains his remark to Degas that verse is made not out of ideas, but of words. Whereas words were traditionally conceived as symbols which unveiled the mystery of things, now things "do their own thing" ["céder l'initiative aux mots"].[75] But these "things" only bear the traces of Mallarmé's mode of perceiving reality as non-being. He will say "There is no reality left; it has evaporated into writing."[76] This judgment would later be extended by Beckett: "There is nothing to express, nothing with which to express, nothing from which to express, no desire to express—together with the obligation to express."[77]

In his prose poem "The White Water-Lily," Mallarmé imagines himself rowing a boat onto the estate of a woman friend. Although he thinks he hears her footsteps, he refuses to look up, preferring her imagined face to reality. Silently and without a glance, he swings the boat around and rows away, explaining:

> So vague a concept is sufficient to itself; it will not transgress that delight imbued with generality which both allows and demands the exclusion of all faces . . .
>
> [Si vague concept se suffit: et ne transgressera le délice empreint de généralité qui permet et ordonne d'exclure tous les visages . . . ][78]

The genteel teacher of English "will deny the world, set up this Absence within it, and identify himself with it. *He who was once denied* turns into the Denier. Revolt is ineffectual, inconceivable, impractical; but refusal is possible. Even though his refusal will be expressed with much politeness and ceremoniousness, with a kind of elegant good humor, it will be *all inclusive.*"[79] He is bent on annihilation.

My hunger which feasts here on no fruit
Finds in their learned absence an equal flavor.

[Ma faim qui d'aucun fruits ici ne se régale
Trouve en leur docte manque une saveur égale.][80]

In this dereistic process Mallarmé almost does away with himself. For nights on end, as his wife and child lie sleeping in the next room, he contemplates suicide; but an improbable project alters his plan. He will "convert his personal failure into the Impossibility of Poetry; and then, in yet another reversal, he will transform the Failure of Poetry into a Poetry of Failure."[81]

For Mallarmé, poetry becomes the sole means of tempering his death wish. "Literature exists alone, to the exception of everything else."[82] Like Hofmannsthal's Lord Chandos, he yearned for a language "of which not a single word is known to me, a language in which mute objects speak to me and in which I shall one day, perhaps in the grave, have to give account of myself before an unknown judge."[83]

Mallarmé hoped that he might one day discover a secret idiom which would voice "that Nothingness which is the Truth."[84] His abstruseness, his aversion to ordinary poetic discourse, his "well-mannered terrorism"[85] (he once said that the only kind of bomb he knew was a book[86]), conspired to make "that Nothingness" more real than life itself: "The Work of Art, through the agency of Man, and Man, through the agency of the Work of Art, draw themselves out of Nothingness."[87]

The poet's negative vision abolishes everything: lace, bed, flight of the swan, ptyxis. "What is involved here," says Sartre, "is not the mere absence of a particular being, but a 'resonant disappearance'; one in which every absence opens onto a more all-embracing and more universal absence until finally, just as language in poetic form returns to the world, the whole world disappears from language."[88]

Mallarmé's written poems—calling cards from the living dead—stand in lieu of "The Book, for I'm convinced that there is only one [Book] . . . the Orphic explanation of the Earth which is the poet's sole responsibility and the true function of literature."[89]

When Mallarmé yearned for a linguistic transparency where

words would "take light from mutual reflection like an actual trail
of fire over precious stones,"[90] he elucidates his own idea that all
poetry had gone wrong since the great Homeric deviation. Like
Heidegger, he extolls the epiphanic quality of language, but
whereas Heidegger invokes Heraclitus, Mallarmé appeals to
Orpheus—who left no written legacy.[91]

A letter of Ludwig Wittgenstein's, written some twenty years after the poet's death, shows the extent to which this notion had
infiltrated modernist theory: "My work consists of two parts: the
one presented here [the *Tractatus*] plus all that I have not written.
And it is precisely the second part which is the important one."[92]

Mallarmé, like Yeats's "blind man battering blind men," once said
that "the world is made to end in a book."[93] In rejecting this "blind
man's ditch,"[94] he needed to wrench language from its roots and
poetry from concrete referents. This meant *defamiliarization* by
means of a studied mixture of freshness and sophistication. His
methods—reciprocal negation, multivalency, grammatical disloca-
tions—confiscate identity by promoting a rapid oscillation between
possibilities of meaning. This was his way of assaulting the petrified
façade of established discourse and of bringing to an end the unholy
alliance between world and word. "Mallarmé," declared Sartre in
1960, "must have been very different from the way he is usually
portrayed—passionate, furious. And so much a master of himself
that he had the power to kill himself by a simple movement of the
glottis. It seems to me that his commitment, social as well as poetic,
could not have been greater."[95]

All notes at the end of Sartre's text are from the French edition,
with the exception of the translator's notes, which are marked
(TRANS.). Footnotes at the bottom of the page are those of Jean-
Paul Sartre, save for an occasional note by the translator (TRANS.)
added to facilitate identification of references which may be obscure to the English-speaking reader.

*Mallarmé,*
*or the Poet of Nothingness*

# I

# The Atheist Heritage[1]

In 1848 the fall of the monarchy blows the bourgeoisie's cover;[2] then and there Poetry loses its two traditional themes: Man and God.

First, God: Europe had just received some staggering news, contested by some today: "GOD   DEAD   STOP   INTESTATE." When it came time to take inventory of the estate, panic ensued. What had the deceased left behind? Some haphazard remains that included, among others, Man. Divested of his privileged status that had previously been underwritten by Divine Will, Man vainly sought within himself what François Mauriac called "that part of the creature on whom God had left his imprint."[3] Farewell, Creation, over which man had been appointed shepherd.

Nature—that loathesome creature of 1793[4]—was back on stage. Now older and hardened, it no longer even offered those comforting vestiges of finality that once had justified the high hopes of the revolutionaries. Analytic reason—that most potent of bourgeois weapons—after demolishing the monarchy's grand syntheses, quietly and unwittingly did away with the ultimate crowning synthesis: Self-caused Being, a whole that produces and governs its parts. The universe had come apart. Nature had become nothing more than an infinite dance of dust particles. Beneath life's smooth chemical processes, man began to suspect his true mineral nature.

The bourgeoisie was horrified by this involuntary parricide, just as their grandfathers had been after they had executed Louis XVI. They had the feeling that an unpardonable crime had just been committed and each one tried to shift the blame onto his neighbor. To no avail: the bourgeoisie had to face up to the fact that it had always harbored the crime within itself, and that killing its king had been tantamount to killing its God. Indeed, the bourgeoisie itself *was* the death of God.

The concept of atheism, a constituent part of bourgeois ideology, was perfected with the establishment of bourgeois rule. Henri Guillemin accurately observed that "when the generation after Louis XVIII and Charles X came of age, the de-Christianization of France, cultivated by the intellectual milieux of the end of the Ancien Régime, spread like wildfire to all social classes, despite the pressures of official Christianity. This collapse, this evaporation of the Christian faith, which took place in many French families under the Empire and even under the Restoration, is a historical fact of enormous consequence."[5] Indeed, under the Restoration, de-Christianization had been spreading; by the time of Louis Philippe it had already become a *fait accompli.* The new generation of bourgeois could not lose its faith, for it had none to lose. All it could do was measure the extent of the disaster.

Only then did Universal Absence begin to make itself felt. The parents, too much involved in the struggle, could not see beyond their own deliverance. But the children, gritting their teeth, took stock of the consequences. They would need all the Divine Power they could muster to shore up their self-confidence and to protect themselves from the populace. But their profligate fathers had left them without the succor of religion. Human beings, as ephemeral and finite modes of blind matter, now were obliged to abandon all hope of distinguishing themselves from other molecular structures. If the universe is now nothing more than a jumble of atoms, where is the basis for a moral order?

How can a social hierarchy exist if humanity is merely a species? How can there be a superior Elite if the Higher is to be explained in terms of the Lower? How can resignation still be preached? And the virtues of suffering? If happiness is not available in the next world, how can one possibly answer those who insist on being happy in this one? God drags down with him the very gravediggers who had dug his tomb. Barante writes that "The Evil is in Society,"[6] and Molé that "the foundations of society have been laid bare."[7] Will they try to recover their lost beliefs? But that would mean going backwards. Deep down, they know that the past cannot begin again. Although they sometimes feign belief on appropriate occasions, they are aware that their profession of faith is in bad faith. With horror, the bourgeoisie discovers its real mission: to abolish the aristocracy and then to annihilate itself so that, from its ashes, an unknown social order might be born. It was merely a bridge—a *middle* class in time and space.

The wrath of the poets was awesome. The most violent immediately proclaimed their hatred of Man, that impostor whose grievous fault consisted in not being the son of God. Flaubert set things in motion: "Without ever having, thank God, suffered at their hands, I loathe my fellow beings."[8] But Leconte de Lisle went even further,[9] and in a state of great agitation wrote:

> Man, heir of man and of his accrued evils
> With your dead planet and your vanished Gods,
> Fly away, vile dust . . .*[10]

or even:

> Men, you killers of Gods, the time is not far off
> When . . . you will perish like beasts . . .†[11]
>
> ("To the Moderns")

He readily deplored:

> The shame of thinking and the horror of being a man.‡[12]

They couldn't have made things any clearer: "Kill our Gods! Then what? What will become of us? Such things are inadmissible." Whether they were dispirited by their skepticism or claimed to take pride in it, they all bore the same grudge against their families: they

---

*Homme, héritier de l'homme et de ses maux accrus,
  Avec ton globe mort et tes Dieux disparus,
  Vole, poussière vile . . .
†Hommes, tueurs de Dieux, les temps ne sont pas loin
  Où . . .
  Vous mourrez bêtement . . .
              ("Aux Modernes")
‡La honte de penser et l'horreur d'être un homme.

had been *turned into* atheists, they had *undergone* de-Christianization before they reached the age when they could decide for themselves. To be sure, parents had always chosen their children's religion without consulting them, but at least the children were then free to lose their faith. The young men of mid-century, however, complained of a still more serious intrusion on their freedom: without being consulted, they had been baptized into unbelief. But you cannot lose your atheism the way you lose your faith. And as a matter of fact, every subsequent movement to "return to Christ" preserved the very unbelief it professed to overcome. From 1850 on, faith is the negation of the negation. Nothing can save us from inhabiting a world foresaken by God; if someone still wishes to believe in Him, it will be *despite* His absence (the cynic would say it is *because* of it); and if one obstinately insists on predicting the ultimate triumph of Religion, it is only after acknowledging its devastating defeat.

Now the poets of 1850[13] felt to the very marrow of their bones the cleavage produced by the extraordinarily swift advance of irreligion in European history. They are witnesses of this irreparable breach as well as its first victims. As children, they had been raised on the poems of Lamartine, Hugo, and Vigny and conceived their own futures on the model of those glorious careers. Twenty years earlier, Poetry had no doubt it was a form of knowledge; the poet read the Truth in the stars. Granted, there were a few atheists among the Romantics, but even for them, God was not *dead;* He simply didn't exist. They dispensed with the divine person and clung to the concept of a Divine Idea. No one questioned such things as absolute Truth, Beauty and Good; no one doubted the Poet's Mission. In short, they troubled themselves so little with reasoning that they were content to let belief and disbelief lie side by side, like good bedfellows. Baudelaire, whom both halves of the century could claim, was an expert in dishonesty, drawing on God to supply his intimate ecstasies while denying his existence. Vigny, himself sometimes so close to agnosticism, pitted the infallible intuition of poetic madness against discursive knowledge:

> If poetic madness is sacred and can be so conceived, isn't it because the recollection of divine things, known by our souls before birth, becomes so vivid that we seem to be drawn back

into the very bosom of Divinity? Haven't we realized that reason is an equally effective weapon in the hands of Truth? Thus we can be confident of having attained the True, the Good and the Beautiful only during those precious moments when our soul, remembering heavenly beauty, takes wing and journeys back to it. Once our soul clearly beholds beauty on every side, it feels penetrated by its love and cannot henceforth look upon anything in the universe that is not illuminated by the splendors of the Godhead.[14]

But the austere sons of these heedless and prodigal fathers could not help looking reality in the face. For them, neither atheism nor the poet's Calling was one of those notions you think up, but whose real implications only appear later through experience. They were but hand-me-downs from a previous generation, thoughts already thought by other people and viewed with a certain detachment. Yet they could not simply be brushed aside; they had to be taken into account, driven to their logical conclusion, then weighed in the balance. No sooner had these poets started to go about this than they saw the Divine Idea run out of steam, the celestial lights go out, and Platonic Truth turn into Illusion. Before they even had a chance to comprehend this sleight-of-hand, they had lost everything: the principal subject of their poetic meditations, the guarantee of their genius, their position in society, as well as their livelihood. Until that time, they had thought a beautiful poem an absolute event, a nervous pulsation from the intelligible world. But now they realized that only the gaze of a Supreme Being could impart to their words the infinite breadth to which they aspired. They had turned to their fellow men for eternal glory; but it was now clear that such glory was beyond their power to grant. Science demonstrated that the human race was perishable and that a planetary mishap would suffice to bring history to an abrupt end. Without realizing it, they had been counting on God to perpetuate their memory. And so their poetry, unrooted in reality, remained up in the air. It had only been prayer, an act of grace and sacrifice; but they *no longer believed* in the being to whom they addressed this prayer. With God dead, their words fell back upon themselves, and now only a desperate nominalism remained. If by some chance the sound of their voices might give some pleasure to men, what of it? Men are but dust, their pleasures are but dust, and all returns to Nothingness.

Only one hope remained: If Poetry could stop trying to mirror the intelligible world, would it not, out of its very misfortune, discover a new mission? Wouldn't the *poetic act,* by virtue of its mere existence, be enough to raise a human being above matter? If he could show he had the power to produce, on his own, effects that nature does not produce—that is, irreducible syntheses—then he could wrest himself from Nature. That is what creating means. Only God had the power to do it. But God does not exist: in nature, "nothing is either created or destroyed." What if the poet were to try just the same? There are two ways of affirming oneself against matter: as creature or as creator. The first way is blocked: let's take the second. The hesitations these poets betrayed should be enough to dispel the absurd legend propagated by the diehards of Christianity. No, our grandfathers were not driven to deicide in a frenzy of pride. On the contrary, the Death of God came very close to provoking a rash of suicides. And if, for a brief time, Poetry was tempted to exploit its divine inheritance and try its hand at creation on a much reduced scale, it was because it was forced either to disappear or to prove itself.

The project, however, was scrapped, or rather put off *indefinitely.* For it was just at this time that they started doubting their own poetic vocation. In the good old days, when people still basked in faith, the gift of poetry had been the sign of the natural aristocrat. God had placed his seal on the brows of the elect; one was a poet by divine will. Inspiration was the secular term for Grace. Since a special providence was needed for the fall of a sparrow, one of another sort was needed for each and every word that fell from a poet's lips; and since every action called for supernatural assistance, it would have been inconceivable that this assistance be denied to the Bard of Creation. In short, the poet was only the trumpet; God supplied the breath. It was the divine voice which made the trumpet resound; and the sounds that escaped rose to heaven, leaving the poet giddy and delirious in the process. With the death of God, sacred delirium becomes just another kind of quirky obsession. It can be artificially stimulated through alcohol; a beautiful poem is just a stroke of luck, a fortuitous event whose probability can perhaps be calculated. The poet is merely a grotesque tin horn[15] that echoes the discordant noises of Nature. His spite drives him to condemn inspiration in all its forms. It so happens that at this very time a foreign poet had just been translated:[16] "His two great enemies are all that is incomprehensible and the result of chance. . . . His genius is passionately taken up with analysis, permutations, and combinations."* And this poet will provide the rules *for composition* which obviate, from the outset, any recourse to "divine delirium." "My next thought concerned the choice of an impression, or effect to be conveyed: and here I may as well observe that, throughout the construction, I kept steadily in view the design of rendering the word *universally* applicable."†

As a direct consequence of the disappearance of the Divine Word, Poetry becomes a technique. I cannot help seeing in this preoccupation with producing effects a sign of hostility toward the public. In the days when the poet sang, his enthusiasm had swept his audience along: they shared communion. Deprived of their God, these poets wish to act on their readers conveying emotions they do not feel; coldly and impassively, they manipulate their readers, contemptuous of the magic spell whose mechanism they understand only too well. This turns out to be a boon for Leconte de Lisle. If poets had continued relying on obscure powers, this unfortunate man would not have long succeeded in concealing his total insignificance. A fart in a soap bubble doesn't offend the nose immediately; but at some point the bubble has to burst. He had the good sense to lay down a rigid doctrine; he managed to impose on two generations the most thankless of tasks.[17] Fifteen years later, a young man named Paul Verlaine, just out of the Lycée, marvelously gifted and extraordinarily lazy, was still trying to write according to this doctrine—but not without a trace of masochism:

> Ah! Superb and sovereign Inspiration . . .
> The Dove, the Holy Spirit, Holy Delirium,
> Opportune Troubles, Obliging Transports,
> Gabriel and his lute, Apollo and his lyre,

*Baudelaire, Preamble to his translation of *The Raven*.
†Poe, *The Philosophy of Composition*.

Ah! Inspiration—one invokes it at sixteen!
What we all need, Supreme Poets
Who venerate the Gods and who don't believe in them . . .
We who chisel words like beakers
And who write moving lines very coldly . . .
Are Willfulness and Will-Power. . . .
What we all need is work without respite,
Unheard-of effort, supreme struggle . . .*[18]

             ("Epilogue III")

It would be difficult to find a more fitting illustration of the bonds that unite inspiration and faith. Verlaine renounces both. But what will come of such austere labor? Creation at long last? That would be going too far. They claim that they are merely *chipping away,* that they are using their Thoughts "like chisels to sculpt the virgin stone of Beauty."[19] But what sort of *Work of Art* does this produce? Is putting a human stamp on matter enough to warrant the name creation? Shouldn't matter and form be created simultaneously, in a single flash of inspiration? The question goes unanswered. None of these poets was arrogant enough to proclaim himself a creator, and none of them had the courage to admit that creation remained off-limits. They waited.

Can we call these diligent workmen atheists? Certainly not. They are immersed in spiritual light. Believers then? No, not that either. They are God's orphans. They experience the Great Shipwreck[20] as a kind of mutilation. Totally at sea on earth, they have no idea why they were born and hate their own contingency. Sometimes they sense within them the stirrings of a vague superfluous life

---

*Ah! l'inspiration superbe et souveraine . . .
La colombe, le Saint-Esprit, le saint Délire,
Les Troubles opportuns, les Transports complaisants,
Gabriel et son luth, Apollon et sa lyre,
Ah! l'inspiration, on l'invoque à seize ans!
Ce qu'il nous faut à nous, les Suprêmes Poètes
Qui vénérons les Dieux et qui n'y croyons pas . . .
A nous qui ciselons les mots comme des coupes
Et qui faisons des vers émus très froidement . . .
C'est l'Obstination et c'est la Volonté. . . .
Ce qu'il nous faut à nous, c'est l'étude sans trêve,
C'est l'effort inouï, le combat nonpareil . . .

whose superabundance horrifies them; at other times they feel that a subtle kind of death has infiltrated men and things, most particularly Poetry. These shamefaced unbelievers, far from scorning the illusions of the older generation, feel petty and small alongside the great bards of romanticism. It wouldn't take much for them to admit that they belonged to a generation of stillbirths. They have neither the swagger of the Titans of 1830 nor the scornful bitterness of Baudelaire. It goes without saying that they didn't dare call themselves bards. The fact of the matter is they even lack the courage to proclaim themselves *poètes maudits*. If they complain, it is only in whispers. No going on about great maledictions or eternal damnation. They are simply jinxed. They feel outmoded, soured, lacking in spirit. They proclaim themselves:

Old . . .
Unhappy without the pride of an austere lack of fortune . . .
These Hamlets thrive on minor discomforts . . .*[21]

("The Jinx")

Do they at least have it in them to feel great passions? Not even that:

They covet hatred and feel only rancor.†[22]

("The Jinx")

They are the Saturnian poets, born under an unlucky star. They have:

A good share of misery and a good share of bile.
A strained and foolish imagination
Comes to obliterate in them the efforts of Reason.
The blood in their veins, subtle as poison,

---

*Vieux . . .
Malheureux sans l'orgueil d'une austère infortune . . .
Ces Hamlets abreuvés de malaises badins . . .
(Mallarmé: "Le Guignon")
† Ils convoitent la haine et n'ont que la rancune.
(Mallarmé: "Le Guignon")

> Hot as lava, and rare, runs and flows,
> Shrivelling up their sad and crumbling Ideal.*[23]
> ("Wise Men of Old Times")

Yet this child of mid-century still needs to sing. What should he sing about? Well, the very same things that had inspired the previous generation—but this time without the inspiration. Whereas they had adored God's presence, he shall deplore His Absence. They had depicted a Universe glowing with Divine Light; he shall portray a world where this light is extinguished, a world in shadow. They had offered thanks to Providence for the fullness within their hearts; he shall indict the whole world for the emptiness he feels inside himself. They had sung the praises of the intelligible world, of Beauty, of absolute Truth—alongside such supreme realities, the most voluptuous smells and the most vivid colors sometimes seemed to be mere dreams; like them, he shall also speak about the Beautiful and the Ideal, but for him it is the Absolute which seems but a dream. Matter alone is identified with truth. God is his incurable wound. He bares it for all to see. Sometimes his body goes so far as to even mimic the void in his soul. The experience of the death of God becomes a benign form of tuberculosis.

In short, the poet has at last found his favorite theme: non-being. Is it to satisfy his resentment? Of course. He calls science and his forebears to the witness stand; this is what you have made of me! Even Parnassian poets are not without a certain amount of exhibitionism.[24] Although Leconte de Lisle's impassiveness may hide his feelings of love, it cannot conceal his spite. But there is more to it than that: these young men are self-appointed penitents. They have the feeling that the tragedy being enacted between Heaven and Earth calls for a human sacrifice for which they are the chosen victims. They resolved that this sacrifice should be a voluntary one,

---

*Bonne part de malheur et bonne part de bile.
 L'Imagination, inquiète et débile,
 Vient rendre nul en eux l'effort de la Raison.
 Dans leurs veines le sang, subtil comme un poison,
 Brûlant comme une lave, et rare, coule et roule
 En grésillant leur triste Idéal qui s'écroule.
                    (Verlaine: "Les Sages d'autrefois")

that their illness must be incurable so that their whole life might be one long period of mourning.

One might ask for whom this mourning and sacrifice are carried on. The bourgeoisie could not care less about despairing poets: if it is terrified by deicide, it is for quite different reasons. The people do not read them. Perhaps God is their only audience? But He is the very one they are mourning! Then who *will* be able to bear witness? They themselves have no idea. Yet it seems to them that their renunciation has a sort of mystical effect on the universe and that, should they ever stop saying no, Matter would become even more material and man even more of a cipher. Through his nostalgia for the Infinite, Baudelaire already thought he could prove that he had gone beyond his worldly state, and that perhaps there was a possibility that, beyond this world, there existed something like an infinite, absolute, and eternal reality. The "Saturnian" poets are more modest. Their dissatisfaction isn't meant to prove anything; they don't make even the most indirect claim for God's existence; yet stubbornly, they keep on insisting that He *ought* to exist. A strange way to go about things, you might say. After all, He either exists or He doesn't. One may still doubt: "*Universal doubt . . .* conforms to the Creator's plan, since He has remained mute in the face of our cries and wished that man have no certain knowledge of Him."* One may still hope and despair! Yet how can they maintain that God obviously does not exist and in the very same breath declare that He ought to? I realize that it is difficult to sustain such an attitude; yet upon reflection, I see in it the beginnings of that large-scale rearguard action leading in the long run to the sophistries of M. le Senne.[25] You start by affirming that the Absolute ought to exist and you end up by defining the Absolute as Value. Or else, like Simone Weil,[26] that God's omnipresence is the same as His universal absence. This should not be viewed as merely attesting to the virulent spread of disbelief; it represents, rather, a Christian strategy which, *after the triumph of atheism,* aims to turn defeat into victory.

The poets I'm speaking about didn't go quite that far. Yet, without fully realizing it, they held that Ideal Being was a more tenuous

---

*Alfred de Vigny, *Journal d'un Poète.*

(and hence more spiritualized) form of Existence than Actual Being. No, God does not exist; and if men would only sacrifice themselves and show by their *spleen* that He *ought* to exist, then something might still be salvaged from the wreckage. But perhaps atheism was the ultimate trial God had inflicted on them? The Almighty wished that "man should have no certain knowledge of Him," but nevertheless He bestowed on him the gift of faith: He wanted Job to undergo every possible form of suffering, yet still remain faithful. Isn't it possible that today He has arranged the universe in such a way that everything conspires to convince us of His death? In that case the true believers, unable to refute the overpowering arguments of materialism, would recognize one another through their common despair. They would constantly proclaim the stupidity of the world, and would demonstrate by their freely accepted *decline* that Man without God is impossible. This self-destruction, which goes beyond atheism, would then be a kind of proof by the absurd, against all evidence, of divine Reality. Conscious or not, this attempt to base their appeal to God on His death can only be understood in a climate of defeat. These atheists are forerunners, and their poetry is at the root of the neo-Christianity so widespread today and which I would call: a faith which courts failure. Or, if you prefer, poetry courts failure in order to experience the pangs of Religion's failure. But since, at the same time, their disbelief is sincere and final, since Rage and Resentment drive these poets to outbid both materialism and the refutations of the freethinkers, it is only fitting to call this ambiguous attitude, so contradictory and so impossible to pin down, the infantile disorder of atheism.[27]

But the disaster did not end there. The failure of religious Poetry was paralleled by a failure of social poetry. At the very time the bourgeoisie was losing both its monarch and its God, it caught a glimpse of the class struggle taking place behind its own factional rivalries. People were already talking openly about "the great February catastrophe."[28] As early as 15 August 1848, *La Revue des Deux Mondes* prayed: "May force . . . be on our side." All the propertied classes, Proudhon wrote, "had sworn hatred for the Republic."[29] It would turn over all its political rights to a gang of strong-arm men who in return would guarantee their right to property.

Literature, of course, is muzzled. Isn't the writer himself a member
of the bourgeoisie? Consequently, like everyone else, he has relin-
quished his rights—particularly the right to speak his mind. It matters little that he didn't personally sign the contract since his entire
class signed for him. And if in fact he doesn't have—or doesn't
always have—a large fortune to protect, it is equally true that he has
a very special interest in the maintenance of order; we could
scarcely expect him to harken to the murmurings of his genius if an
iron fist had not previously silenced the turmoil outside.

In the civil war which is brewing and which will silently be led by
specialists, agitators, and politicians, the poet will play the busy-
body. Whichever side he takes, he need only raise his voice and his
partisans are compromised. Let him be content to amuse and edify.
If he goes beyond this he'll be dragged into court. Once the operation is brilliantly executed, the patient, relieved of his rights, picks
himself up and brushes himself off, feeling somewhat embittered
and not very proud of himself. He feels he has been both victim
and accomplice; he loses himself in a new set of problems: How
should he decide whether literature should favor a doctrine of
order or freedom? He already starts anticipating an argument of
later invention, that excellent way of getting poets to accept dictatorship: "Our literature was never more French than when it was most
policed and most rigidly controlled. . . . This control, far from
crushing the individual, in fact uplifts him." Besides, what did he
gain from the triumph of the rabble? It didn't make up his public.
Of course, an artist must despise the deicidal bourgeoisie. Yet, it is
they, after all, who create and nourish him. Better to stick with this
unspeakable class, reserving the right to cover it with opprobrium,
than to push it into the abyss and so risk sliding into it oneself.

All the same, the poet has a bad conscience. Like the hero of
Schiller's *The Brigands*,[30] he willingly would have opposed the law
of his heart to the contemptible march of the world, if only he
weren't afraid of finding the world once again in the depths of his
heart. General retreat of poetry. Order of the day: lie low, wait,
beware. It was to stay on the defensive until the end of the century.
The time would seem propitious for soul-searching. But will the
poet now search his soul? Not just yet: for the time being, he sulks:

Today, Action and Dream broke
The primitive Pact worn down by the centuries . . .
Force, which the Poet formerly held
In rein, Force, a winged white horse that shone,
Force is now the Ferocious Beast . . .*[31]

("Prologue")


Hero of a great lost battle, that great Patriarch, Victor Hugo, is on his Island.[32] His sons view his exile as a symbol of defeat, more glorious than victory itself—one consecrating the recent separation of the Temporal from the Spiritual. From their position on the Continent, they will attempt to commune, through a sort of mystical complicity, with his commanding Absence. They will model themselves on It, speak for It, live by It; they will draw everyone's attention to It by their airs and attire. Father and Sons are both equally mad. The former takes himself to be Poetry-in-Exile, while the others claim to embody the Exile of Poetry. Later, when the Patriarch returns, he announces the return of Poetry to the World. But his sons turn a deaf ear; for them, Exile has become second nature. The Absence of the Father, their own Absence from the world, and the eternal Absence of God merge into a sort of Trinity, each of whose terms serves to vindicate the other two. Hugo in defeat is equated with the death of God. In His dangerous world, the Poet was doomed to fail. By their aimlessness and apathy the sons will demonstrate that God, Man, and Poetry are all equally impossible. A Parisian City Hall clerk by the name of Paul Verlaine gives away the ending of this comic opera:


*Aujourd'hui, l'Action et le Rêve ont brisé
  Le Pacte primitif par les siècles usé . . .
  La Force, qu'autrefois le Poète tenait
  En bride, blanc cheval ailé qui rayonnait,
  La Force, maintenant, la Force, c'est la Bête
  Féroce . . .
                    (Verlaine: "Prologue")

. . . Behold the chorus of Poets . . .
The world, troubled by their profound words,
Commits them to exile. They, in turn, will exile the world.*[33]

("Prologue")

This indiscreet *finale* gives the entire game away. It is simply a matter of reversing terms. In every case it is taken for granted that the Negative stands for the Positive. The poet claims to be the one who gives coherence to the misfortunes he passively endures,[34] and he recognizes, in the very restrictions imposed on him, evidence of his elect status. With an air of affectation, he deferentially keeps within the limits that have been set for him. He makes a point of stubbornly refusing to give up his seat while in reality he is really being forced to remain in it. This sullen attitude, which makes obedience a challenge and passivity an act of insubordination, they call *dignity*. Proudly, the poet holds his tongue, since in fact no one asks him to speak. Not quite—he will write—but only to proclaim that he is holding his tongue. Are there certain things he is not supposed to mention? Very well, he won't talk about *anything*. From 1860 to 1900, literature goes on a silence strike.[35] I don't think the public even noticed.

When the older generation wrote, it was to take delight in their own prodigality. Poetry had become the highest form of generosity; the milk from its ever-flowing breast was valued more for its abudance than for its quality. Heredia will say about Lamartine: "Day in and day out, he is as unsparing of his life as he is of his genius. . . . He gives his all, he gives himself—Nature made him a patrician. His concern for the people is but the ultimate generosity of his great soul."[36] After 2 December everything changes.[37] Even the most prolific writers have trouble turning out one volume every ten years. Such widespread impotence can hardly be ascribed to an individual's character; it can only be seen as a feature of the period. It is certainly a result of irreligion. Far from inspiring a return to

* . . . Voici le groupe des Chanteurs . . .
Le monde, que troublait leur parole profonde,
Les exile. A leur tour ils exilent le monde!
(Verlaine: "Prologue")

the pagan cult of Nature, the death of God gives rise to an atheistic Manicheanism in which the Gnostic distinction between Light and Darkness is replaced by the opposition between Nothingness and Being. With the disappearance of Being-in-Itself, the infinite collection of beings is lost in a sea of contingency; each one might just as well not be, or might just as well be other than itself. For our Atheists-in-Spite-of-Themselves, all that exists reflects back on the vain and absurd image of their being. In every pebble, in every rose, they perceive their own perfect incongruity. They begin to call this direct intuition of Being *ennui*. Besides, if God does not exist, Being and matter become interchangeable terms; Being is dispersion, inertia, and exteriority.

The poet despises this brute Matter which reduces him to purely random dispersal. It challenges all privileges. This unbearable egalitarianism brazenly taunts Hero, Genius, and Saint with the evidence that "all forms of being are alike."[38] Being, Matter, Nature, the Natural—four terms the Saturnian Poets scornfully lump together—serve only to express, each in its own way, the mute democracy of all things. The poet hates Woman, who is "natural—therefore vulgar";[39] he hates any sort of burgeoning or blossoming—anything, in fact, that seems to add being to being. He fears his own natural instincts as if they belonged to some sort of ape locked up inside him. Tightly buttoned up, starched and stiffened, he refuses to let go in any way. What could he succumb to if not to Nature? Now he curbs his enthusiasm and smothers his desires, since gratification is fullness and all fullness is a fullness of being. As much as he hates woman for her "moist and rounded forms," he hates the male for his sweat, his hair, his gamy smell. Rather than just being themselves, they prefer to play a role. This way they can at least be sure of having created a role which has the added advantage of not being real.

This cult of artifice frequently leads them to adorn themselves with an abstract femininity. Like homosexuals, they loathe woman's carnal reality, yet are attracted by the Idea of femininity; this way they can simply play at being what they cannot be and deny what they are. Their effusiveness, their swooning, their cloying sweetness—all these antics might make people take them for queers. But no. With rare exceptions, they didn't engage in homosexuality. They were rather more likely to be cold and impotent, occasionally stirred by a brief onset of priapism for which they would inevitably repent. Most of the time they indulged in a surface eroticism of unfeeling fingers and words. In a word, they were teases.

One understands why they were horrified by the fertility of romanticism. The prolific geniuses of 1830[40] were perpetually giving birth, engendering indifferently, amid slime and excrement, living offspring, monsters, and stillbirths. What was the point of devoting oneself to Art if you were only going to end up back in the midst of Nature? Wasn't there a danger of mistaking the poem for the honey and the poet for the bee? How dreadful! They would replace this vulgar prodigality with a carefully measured sterility. Poetry now gives up large-scale production and devotes itself to quality. In place of the unbridled abundance of its predecessors who had wound up causing verbal inflation, it substitutes an aesthetics of scarcity. They now specialize in luxury goods. Constricted to the point of constipation, the newcomers jealously conceal their poems from indifferent crowds. To ward off prying fingers, they put golden clasps[41] on their books: the public is requested not to touch. One writes principally for oneself, then for one's fellow poets, and finally for a few collectors of rare objects. Sometime prior to the invention of the bicycle, we see the appearance of that typically French tandem: Avarice and Literature. There had, of course, always been misers who wrote; but never before this *fin de siècle* did one write *in order* to be a miser.

The real aim of all this is to restore an aristocracy. Science had not been content to kill God and abolish the Ideal; through reasoning and experience it established truths accessible *to everyone*. It declares that "Good sense is of all things in the world the most equally distributed."[42] In revealing "the evidence that all forms of existence are equal,"[43] science destroys the objective basis of all hierarchy. By holding that Truth can be conveyed, it destroys the negative basis of inequality. Everyone agrees, bourgeois and poet alike, that the inroads of public education are deplorable. "There is one thing," writes Montalembert, "which grows in France along with the progress of universal primary education: crime."[44] Flaubert, like Leconte de Lisle, can never stop railing against it. Even the gentle Lefébure, postal clerk and future archeologist, is only

one among thousands who writes: "We don't have enough backward people."[45] But what if there were more of them, if France
were steeped in illiteracy, would things be any better? The damage
has already been done, for agitators have persuaded the people
that they are capable of learning and that only poverty and the bad
faith of the ruling class deprives them of it.

The bourgeoisie couldn't have cared less about the problem of
ignorance. It was in their vital interest to pronounce it incurable.
Unstable and contradictory, a product of history wanting to call a
halt to history, the bourgeoisie would preach equality against its
former masters, while proclaiming its own natural superiority
against the slaves. Here, then, is the end result of the analytic spirit:
the bourgeoisie liquidates itself and will be absorbed into the popular classes or the aristocracy; it will be swallowed up in universal
equivalency unless it can somehow manage to reestablish for its
own benefit the synthetic spirit which, along with its irreducible
absolutes, had been so badly defeated in 1789. Its attitude toward
the proletariat is ambiguous: it would like to break down that enormous, indigestible lump, the Masses, to pulverize them into power-
less individuals. Even as it denies the existence of those synthetic
entities called social classes, it hopes to persuade the workers, by
subtle allusions to ineffable certainties and revealed truths, that
there exists a hierarchy of souls. In brief, they must be reminded
on every possible occasion that there are innate differences among
men. The bourgeoisie speaks neither of blood nor of breeding but
alludes casually to tact, to good taste, to the *esprit de finesse*, and to all
such other qualities which cannot be acquired. When a "superior"
class sees its superiority challenged, it defends itself by a resort to
the esoteric, all the while keeping open the option of bloodier and
more effective measures.

The disconcerting "rise" of the bourgeoisie was certainly at the
origin of troubadour poetry. I don't believe that we need to see in
courtly love either a transposition of the Albigensian heresy[46] or
even the Cult of the Virgin. Rather, it was a defensive reaction on
the part of feudal lords who idealized their relationship to their
vassals and projected it onto a Platonic heaven. Similarly, at a time
when the nobility was battling on two fronts, the Précieux movement served as a diversionary tactic. Those who attacked the

Marquise de Rambouillet's *salon* made a brilliant but futile attempt to shift the scene of the battle to the cultural arena. And Preciosity[47] is just what the bourgeoisie of 1850 needs; since it claims to be irreplaceable, it must try to justify itself; and if everyone is supposed to be capable of thought, the élite must hint at realities so subtle, with so many variegated articulations which, by their very nature, must remain inaccessible to scientific reason, yielding their secrets only to a few extraordinarily privileged souls. Unless one is born with the requisite intuitive capacity, not even a lifetime of study will suffice to acquire it. In short, since Reason has risen against established authority, since it has become the great leveler, the bourgeoisie will turn to the Irrational and fall back, as usual, on the reasons of the heart. On every issue and on every occasion it will keep the aristocratic spirit alive as a form of permanent agitation. It would not be wrong to call this persistence of the notion of hierarchy a "permanent counter-revolution." This notion must be aired on all occasions, whether in the columns of the official press, in the eloquence and wit of a member of the Académie Française, or in the declarations of a minister or a general. It is at the root of that bourgeois brand of Manicheanism known as "distinction." Never called by its rightful name, yet always implied, the absolute superiority of the bourgeoisie is the other side of its egalitarian declaration.

Once again, the poets act as agents of the "Précieuse" counter-revolution. In all sincerity they would like to "distinguish" themselves from the bourgeoisie. But wasn't the latter trying to distinguish itself from the people? Whatever the poets do against it, the bourgeoisie turns to its own advantage. Their predecessors had proclaimed themselves seers and prophets. But that was an age when animals spoke and books were taken down directly from the lips of God. Their godless successors are not only aware that the nobility is gone, but that all men, without exception, are merely useless configurations of matter. Poetry discovers a new mission for itself: to reconstitute, *in the face of the truth,* a phantom Nobility. To oppose the public Truths of Science, it establishes a *realm of the incommunicable*. Beauty becomes its selective principle. Outwardly available to everyone but in reality accessible only to a privileged handful, Beauty, solely by virtue of its existence, has the mission of breaking down the irreducible differences which divide men, and which cause a hierarchical break in society. Above the common herd,[48] a select group of connoisseurs will band together with the artists to establish a knightly order based on poverty and mysticism. This small half-monastic and half-militant spiritual community, whose authority is conferred by the Académie Française, the Société de Pensée, and the Confrérie Religieuse, had its own heroic myth—Predestination—as well as its own initiation rites. Privileged by his misfortunes, the poet exhibits himself in the world through his unhappiness; whereupon he is recognized by his peers, who recruit each other by co-optation. After undergoing the customary initiation rites, he publishes his poems in little magazines.

For several decades, poets only frequented other poets. The gatherings at the home of Leconte de Lisle[49] had the solemnity of a religious service; a strict hierarchy was observed: Victor Hugo was the captive King; Leconte de Lisle was the Viceroy. In private, they liked calling each other Prince, Duke, or High Constable. They nervously flaunted a kind of symbolic Aryanism as a way of disguising the horrors they felt over their own plebeian origins.* Their totally negative aristocracy is built on the ruins of any kind of aristocratic distinction. They dress up their idle nostalgia for a defunct nobility with noble titles; and their vaunted singularity is really nothing but the negation of universality. This impossible negation, which recognizes itself as such, nevertheless takes pride in affirming itself in the teeth of all evidence.

The setback that poetry underwent in 1851 and the disaster suffered by the French nobility in 1793 reflect and corroborate one another. Both these defeats are the earthly reflection of a metaphysical drama. With its triumph over the nobility and over the poets, the bourgeoisie loses its bearings and kills its God. Dead aristocrats, nobler than they ever were in their lifetimes, enjoy the singular distinction of lying in the grave; neglected poets, anointed by exile,[50] take a princely pride in being unread. These are two aspects of a single reality: the bourgeois ennoble themselves by incarnating the death of the very nobility that had been massacred

---

*Manifestations of this hatred appear as late as Lautréamont: "It appears from what I've been told that I am the offspring of a man and a woman. I find this quite astonishing! I thought I was more than that."[51]

by their grandfathers. A little sleight-of-hand suffices to transform privation into wealth—they adopt the haughty bearing of the Prince, his disdain, his stoicism, and his absence. This brotherhood of initiates has its own mystery: that of the Transubstantiation of Nothingness into Being, No into Yes, Impossibility into Necessity. Carrying this enterprise to its limits, they refuse to live. One particular circumstance makes this refusal easier: they are *poor*.

With reduced material circumstances, the world of Letters attracted a different sort of recruit, something which should come as no surprise to us. A survey of the background of graduates of Saint-Cyr[52] would reveal significant variations in their social origins, depending on whether or not war was held in favor. As long as Poetry paid off,* young men from good families were not above devoting their talents to it. Now muzzled and fallen from grace, it hardly brings in more than the occasional dinner invitation. It loses its appeal; yet for this very reason it suddenly becomes more accessible to the *petit bourgeois* who used to be intimidated by what he considered a pleasure of the rich. As the literary Titans faded into the past, humble souls took heart. Had they persisted in believing that the measure of talent was success, these unfortunates would never have managed to write a single line. But when it became apparent that success had nothing to do with merit, they allowed themselves to dream of a merit which would raise them above success. The fact of the matter is that they endured a life of hardship for over a hundred years.

Until then, God had been the screen concealing the basic absurdity of their humble lives. A thankless existence found its reward and meaning in Heaven, and by zealously carrying out their tasks, the poets could say that they were helping to maintain order in the universe. But to their dismay, de-Christianization caused the scales to fall from their eyes. "Previously," wrote Musset in 1835, "the oppressor said 'The earth is mine,' the oppressed replied, 'Heaven is mine!' Today what would his answer be?"[53] Today . . . that would depend. A member of the working class would claim his place in the sun; he would even strive to conquer it by force. But the *petit bourgeois*, mystified and underpaid, respectful in spite of

---

*In 1848 Victor Hugo's fortune was valued at 180 million francs, 1952 value. Toward the end of his life, his estimated worth was in excess of two billion francs.

himself, demands nothing. He is not a rebel, still less a revolutionary. He does not want to overthrow society. As rich Jews once did in
Poland, and as Blacks in the ex-Congo still do today, he never stops
seeking admission into what are called the "higher circles." A class
which thrives on resentment, proud humility, envy, and gnawing
shame, the *petite bourgeoisie* figures it will have to pay the damages
for the great collisions of History. That's already what they thought
in 1850.

They were wrong—the industrial and agricultural proletariat,
crippled by recent events, would foot the bill. Since the coup d'etat,
the upper and middle bourgeoisies had resumed their rise. The
economic crisis of the previous few years is forgotten and blamed
on revolutionary agitation. Some *petits bourgeois* take part in the
general prosperity; many others, petty tradesmen, modest shopkeepers, had been ruined by big industry and trade; those who
remain know that they will not be able to hold out against the
machine for long. In vain do the small tradesmen and employees
steel themselves to the imperceptible slide which brings them ever
closer to the proletariat. They are aware of their fate; and for this
reason, though they sometimes despise the mighty of this world,
they reserve their full hatred for the working classes who seem so
near.

Nietzsche's well-known aphorism applies to the *petit bourgeois:* "In
every ascetic morality, man adores part of himself as God and to
that end needs to diabolicize the rest."[54] The *petit bourgeois* diabolicizes History, that scourge which periodically ruins him. He
diabolicizes Nature and Life itself because they smack of the rabble.
He contrives to bask in the light that radiates from the ruling
classes and, since he foolishly insists on maintaining an order that
victimizes him, has no recourse other than raising himself above
the crowd in an attitude of affected and sulking negativism. He
must distinguish himself from the workers by his merits. The self-
inflicted privations do not basically stem from his utilitarian principles. He wants to mortify his own sinful flesh. He wants to kill the
worker who breathes and digests with his body. His blind resentment of what he basely calls "the upper crust," his lucid and bitter
consciousness of being inferior, his ambivalent attitude toward the
worldly goods and toward inequality, his total lack of either histori-

cal or class consciousness, his acknowledged complicity with the captains of the ruling class, his excessive eagerness, his punitive self-discipline and self-defeating behavior—all these characteristics constitute, if not the ideology of the *petits bourgeois*—they never had any—then at least their ideological complex.

Up to now, this complex had never inspired poets—except, perhaps, as an object of ridicule, as when they laughed at shopkeepers and cloddish peasants. But all at once Poetry, chained and scorned, becomes their private property. The universe had abandoned it; all they need do is to take possession of it. Up to this time sons asphyxiated by their modest and puritan families had been willing to throttle their hopes and follow in their fathers' footsteps. They had always kept their misery and their feelings of revolt to themselves. But now that Poetry is suddenly available, it becomes an escape from their own bitterness. Exasperated by the father's ultimately pointless puritanism, the son wishes to break free of his roots.

In his resentment he will say no to everything. He heaps scorn on the vulgar rich and on the boorish rabble; he gives voice to his impossible dream of an aristocracy of pure souls. But while he thinks he is opposing his father or his uncle, he is actually following in their footsteps. For him, just as for them, hardship and self-mortification will serve no other purpose than to increase the victim's capacity for holiness. Bureaucrat-father and poet-son alike had decided to conceal their poverty by assuming an air of spirituality. And when the poet scorns the riches he can't acquire, he resembles all those members of his family who thought—and repeatedly insisted—that obedience, modesty, chastity, and the daily performance of one's duties imparted to the poor man's soul a quality that the rich might very well envy. And when he gives himself over to the Absolute, pretending to consider the Ideal as essential and his Ego as inessential, he still resembles his parents, who had irrevocably given themselves over to invisible Capital. It is from them that he gets his taste for purity, his respect for the mighty of this earth; and it is from them that he gets his hatred of Nature and of Life.

In short, the ruin of poetry became emblematic of their own personal failures, endowing these with an unsuspected depth.

They wrote because poetry no longer paid, because the peevish dignity of the petty employee could be confused with the sullen dignity of the unemployed *bard,* and because their unavowable human frustrations could be sublimated in the Poet's righteous resentment. What an admirable way these poets have of grasping the poetic Idea: it incites them to go on a silence strike.[55] This *real* revolt, which pits the Spiritual against the Temporal, is accompanied by their *imaginary* revolt, which pits the humble against the mighty. Thrifty by necessity, these teachers, postal employees, municipal clerks, office managers, and assistant librarians grant themselves the luxury of being stingy by renouncing in advance all the goods they could never afford. " 'Ardèche.' The name horrifies me. And yet it contains the two words to which I have devoted my life: 'Art. Poverty.' "*[56]

Poverty became a providential trial, even a sign of election. "Good, down-to-earth poverty, which dragged me by the scruff of my neck through everything external to my poetic calling, made me . . . weary of base . . . external things."[57] They could easily imagine that their destitution was a product of their asceticism. In short, Poetry, which for the great Romantics was the highest form of generosity, became in the eyes of these modest workmen the Art of considering poverty a luxury. "And as for living?" they asked. "Our servants will do that for us."[58] But they had no servants except, once in a while, a maid whom they extolled as a princess and whom they might marry *in extremis.*[59] Even illness seemed to them a privilege. "What should we be doing here? And what excuse would we have for remaining if we weren't pierced, haunted, fleeced, defamed, and bleeding? We need to be sick; it is our fairest title to enduring nobility."[60] They claim they barely exist: "My heart is embalmed in its own regrets,"[61] one of them said. And another: "I am a sad, wandering soul, a passive spirit adrift among things, an exile in springtime who feels at home in the fall."[62] And again: "The state of our hopes exiles us from earth."[63] Paul Verlaine, not yet out of high school, wrote:

---

*Mallarmé's pun, "*Art. Dèche,*" is untranslatable. Part of the Ardèche region is dry and unproductive. *Dèche* is a slang word for poverty.—TRANS.

I don't believe in God, I abjure and renounce
All thought; as for that old irony,
Love, I'd like to hear no more of it.
Weary of life and in dread of dying, like
A brig adrift, a plaything of the ebb and flow,
My soul sets sail for frightful shipwrecks.*[64]

("Anguish")

These nebulous little souls, always on the verge of fainting, found more spirituality in inertia than in activity. Baudelaire had regretted his failure to unite Dream with Action; his more radical epigones were delighted by it: "One modern poet's foolishness even went so far as to regret that Action was not Dream's sister . . . My Lord! If this were the case . . . where could we hide?"[65] At bottom, this inertia was at once an indictment and a protest of innocence: We haven't done a thing! We're not even guilty of being born. The responsibility rests squarely with society.† This is what I refer to elsewhere as the quietism of resentment. Without actually being drawn to real suicide, they all preferred death to life. Most of them, to spare themselves the extreme torments of a self-inflicted death, decided to be dead even *during* their lifetimes. Corbière rewrote his epitaph several times:

He killed himself out of ardor or died of sloth
If he lives, it is out of obliviousness . . .‡

---

* Je ne crois pas en Dieu, j'abjure et je renie
  Toute pensée et quant à la vieille ironie,
  L'Amour, je voudrais bien qu'o n ne m'en parlât plus.
  Lasse de vivre, ayant peur de mourir, pareille
  Au brick perdu jouet du flux et du reflux,
  Mon âme pour d'affreux naufrages appareille.
  ("Angoisse")
  (See note, p. 121.)
† Tristan Corbière: "They robbed me of my life." ["On m'a
  manqué ma vie."] [Underneath a portrait of Corbière.]
‡ Il se tua d'ardeur, ou mourut de paresse.
  S'il vit, c'est par oubli . . .

And:

> He died waiting to live
> And lived waiting to die.*[66]

The Master entreats us:

> Man! Learn to die before having existed . . .
> Seek in the depths of the tomb, in its reality,
> The secret of life.†[67]

It is wonderful to watch all these corpses jovially competing for the death prize: "Which is the deader of us two? Surely it is I."‡ They adopted all the negative categories of failure and recrimination, preferring Past to Present, Artifice to Nature, Desire to Fulfillment, and Indifference to Desire. They were not in the least upset with the thought that they had missed out on life and even on writing:

> Here lies a heartless heart, badly planted
> Too successful—as a *failure*.§[68]

Sometimes they pushed their dread of created things to the point of declaring (something readily acknowledged today) that their best poems were the ones they hadn't written: "I felt stirring within me . . . the old dead poems of my youth—beautiful for never having been written."‖ To be sure, they were not unaware that the

---

* Il mourut en s'attendant vivre
  Et vécut, s'attendant mourir.
† Homme! sache mourir avant d'avoir été . . .
  Cherche au fond de la tombe en sa réalité
  Le secret de la vie.
‡ From a letter by Lefébure, 15 July 1868. [In Mondor, *Eugène Lefébure*.]
§ Ci-gît—coeur sans coeur, mal planté
  Trop réussi—comme *raté*.
‖ Letter from Lefébure to Mallarmé, 2 March 1865. [In Mondor, *Eugène Lefébure*.]

Aristocracy is an integral part of societies based on lavish consumption, and that the nobleman is a privileged consumer who must, in the name of all, accomplish the ritual destruction of man's worldly goods—while the human race gapes on admiringly as the goods it has created by the sweat of its brow are consumed. But since these aristocratic orgies were beyond their means, they replaced the riotous squandering of wealth by a systematic negation of Reality. In those military and agricultural societies, saints carried destruction to its limits; an entire society saw itself reflected in its glory and in its self-destructive generosity. These poets abjured everything, even basic necessities, yet their prolonged agony is inconceivable in the absence of the luxury and mythology of a society based on consumption. Since they could not be warriors, the poets of 1850 would become saints. In the midst of a commercial and an industrial society, they would bring new luster to the funereal dreams and bygone follies of an extinct community. Moreover, their verbal challenge to Being helps sustain their resentment. They gave a name to this universal negativism: the Dream. We ought not even imagine that their idle musings have any content. There are, of course, exceptions; but on the whole, Dream, Silence, and Sullenness commingle and we can only compare the mental state of these poets to a mild case of schizophrenia without actual delirium.

> —O Brahma! All things are the dream of a dream . . .*
> ("The Vision of Brahma")

or:

> The ultimate Void of Beings and Things
> Is the unique justification of their reality.†
> ("The Secret of Life")

---

*—O Brahma! toute chose est le rêve d'un rêve . . .
(Leconte de Lisle: ["La Vision de Brahma," *Poèmes antiques*])
† Le Néant final des Etres et des Choses
  Est l'unique raison de leur réalité.
(Leconte de Lisle: ["Le Secret de la vie," in *Poèmes antiques*])

And again:

> Void son of the Void, of what do you complain?*
> ("The Pride of the Void")

And here is a revealing admission which shows how their resentment against Everything creeps into their very thirst for knowledge.

> Son of a godless century, without books or apostles,
> At first I sought after the Absolute, like others
> And I began with old age, finding it
> Less necessary to be a man than a man of science.
> I made a great laboratory of my brain . . .
> I pulverised nature in the strange retort
> Of my twisted spirit, which simmered beneath
> *My will to see in a disintegrated universe* . . .†

The fact is that they use Science (or rather Scientism[69]), for achieving two opposing ends: contemporary materialism is the main cause of both their atheism and of their despair. Science, writes Lefébure in 1867,[70] "will open up an unbridgeable gap in the history of human life on earth, before and after Hope, that noble Hope which once lifted man's eyes toward the heavens and which, now that it abandons him, drops him back on all fours." Physics and Physiology reduce the Ideal to an illusion. But it is precisely the resentment this discovery produces that leads them to push this disintegration even further. In fact it was not absolutely necessary that their loss of faith should have

---

*Fils du Néant, néant, de quoi donc te plains-tu?
   (Jean Lahor: ["La Fierté du néant," in *L'Illusion,* 1875–93. Paris: Alphonse Lemerre. Jean Lahor is the pseudonym of one of Mallarmé's close friends, the poet Henri Cazalis.])
†Fils d'un siècle sans Dieu, sans livre et sans apôtres
 J'ai cherché l'Absolu, d'abord, ainsi que d'autres
 Et j'ai commencé par la vieillesse trouvant
 Moins nécessaire d'être un homme qu'un savant.
 J'ai fait de ma cervelle un grand laboratoire . . .
 J'ai broyé la nature en l'étrange cornue
 De mon esprit retors que chauffait par-dessous
 *La volonté de voir dans l'univers dissous* . . .
(Lefébure: [Quoted by Mondor, *Eugène Lefébure*], 95. Sartre's italics.)

driven them back to eighteenth-century analytic materialism.[71] Neo-Kantianism, Agnosticism, Neo-Hegelianism, Relativism, Pragmatism, Dialectical Materialism: all these philosophies would soon arise or had already arisen from the Death of God. But if these dreamers put the worst face on things, it is due to their anguish, moroseness, and design. They have the obscure feeling that along with their entire epoch, they are involved in a great social tragedy which can come to an end only in their lifetimes. One of them refers to the epoch as "a tunnel";[72] and at about this same time Tocqueville gives voice to the widespread sentiment when he writes: "Not only haven't we seen the end of the great revolution that began before our time, but the child born today will probably not see it either. We feel that the old world is coming to an end, but what will the new one be like?"[73] Their bitterness, however, rules out any hope of better days. They prefer the myth of Decadence to the bourgeois myth of Progress. They readily compare themselves to the late Byzantines, or to the Romans of the last days of the Empire. This was their way of acknowledging their desire to yoke their fate to that of the possessing classes. And perhaps as much to disguise the real source of their anguish as to satisfy their rage, they transform the social drama into a cosmic catastrophe. They enjoy imagining the death of the Earth, and find the cooling off of the Sun particularly entertaining:

> A dead world, immense sea foam,
> A gulf of sterile shadows and spectral lights . . .*[74]

Colliding planets aren't bad either:

> . . . the globe and all that lives thereon,
> Lifeless block torn from its immense orbit . . .
> Will stave in its old and miserable crust
> Against some universe immobile in its force . . .†[75]

---

*Un monde mort, immense écume de la mer,
  Gouffre d'ombres stériles et de lueurs spectrales . . .
† . . . le Globe et tout ce qui l'habite,
  Bloc stérile arraché de son immense orbite . . .
  Contre quelque univers immobile en sa force
  Défoncera sa vieille et misérable écorce . . .

With relish they anticipate the terrors of the Last Man on Earth:

> I wandered alone on the Earth, and the Earth was bare;
> Through the endless void, the denuded globe . . .
> Sailed off . . .*[76]

Sometimes, when they wearied of such apocalyptic pronouncements, they moved on to metaphysical annihilation:

> Time, Extension and Number
> Have fallen from the black firmament
> Into the still, dark sea.†[77]

In any event, the method never varies. From some book on popular science they borrow the appropriate weapons to describe the final conflagration. Since science has shown us the emptiness of our Hopes, let us carry its conclusions still further and show the Emptiness of everything. Faced with the prospect of Universal Disaster, the Ideal and the Beautiful through a predictable reversal will emerge as the only admissible truths. Perhaps not enough stress has been laid on the reciprocal negation whereby the Ideal seeks to negate Matter and Matter seeks to negate the Ideal: I personally see this as one of the most striking characteristics of the epoch. In reality, these two Voids are not of the same nature. The one—a pure, multicolored spectrum of ideal qualities—lacks being; the other, once it is divested of the spectrum of colors which our fantasy imparts to it, is reduced to being without qualities. Thus, we are back to the Hegelian dialectic of Being and Non-Being, but as it is experienced. There is absolutely no way of distinguishing pure Being from Non-Being since it is *not anything*. And since we can imagine *Nothingness*, it must at least have a certain degree of being. If—as was then believed—all sensible qualities reveal the nature of

---

*J'errais seul sur la Terre. Et la Terre était nue
  Par le Vide sans fin, le Globe décharné . . .
  S'en allait . . .
† Le Temps, l'Etendue et le Nombre
  Sont tombés du noir firmament
  Dans la mer immobile et sombre.

the senses more than the nature of the object, then every presence—
even the most opaque, the most silent, the most weighty—conceals a
secret absence; being in its pure, naked existence is the negation of
all forms of being; and the mode of being, which is a purely subjective determination, ends up being itself an *appearance*, hence a negation of being.

The poet feels comfortable in the midst of this hall of mirrors.
He repudiates the Dream in the Name of Truth and Being. This is
his lofty despair, his secret suffering, at once corrosive and enno-
bling. He then reestablishes this Dream by bracketing matter in the
name of Ideal Being and Ideal Value. He shifts back and forth
between these two absences, depending on his mood, enjoying either using the one to negate the other or else successively affirming
both of them by moving from despair to a great frenzy of hope, a
hope he knows to be hopeless. In this singular moment of literary
history, the artist no longer believes in art, because he cannot
ground it on divine sanction; but since the entire universe lacks this
sanction, he places his faith in Art alone.

Flaubert was the first writer who oscillated between faith and
doubt in a movement of reciprocal and infinitely circular negation.
Soon they called on Art to "make life vanish."[78] Art appeared to be
no more than an opiate, a bogus substitute for Religion: "The only
way of avoiding unhappiness is to bury oneself in Art without car-
ing for anything else."[79] But "lacking any theological foundation,
on what can this obscure enthusiasm now be based? Some will look
for answers in the pleasures of the flesh, others in old religions, and
still others in art itself."[80] But elsewhere, in far more numerous
and better-known passages, Flaubert affirms his Religion of Art
and declares that his one and only desire is to reach "Truth
through the mediation of the Beautiful."[81]

In Baudelaire there is the same uncertainty. He can write a sonnet on Beauty, or that "all form that has been created, even by man,
is immortal";[82] yet this doesn't keep him from proclaiming, with
the disillusioned wisdom of an Ecclesiastes: "We must work if not
by inclination, then at least out of despair since, when all is said and
done, working is less tedious than amusement."[83] Verlaine, while
still an adolescent, goes even further by publishing, in the same
collection, the following lines:

> I laugh at Art, and Man I laugh at too, and songs
> And verse and old Greek temples . . .*[84]
>
> ("Anguish")

And:

> Oh Don Quixote, . . . your life was a poem,
> And the windmills were wrong, oh my king.†[85]

To get out of this blind alley, someone had to have the courage to follow it to the very end. For the time being, however, these extreme vacillations disturb no one. A thought which accommodates itself so complacently to its own contradictions will find its best expression in Malraux's famous but slightly distorted line: "Art is worth nothing, but nothing is worth Art."‡[86] In "The Secret of Life," Leconte de Lisle expressed the same thought in these terms:

> Yes! Without you, who are nothing, nothing could have been.

Mystified and mystifiers, these poets, whenever they think they are getting away from their social milieu, merely magnify its features. There is no disguising their lowly origins. First of all, their ostentatious and perhaps *overly* strenuous negation of the bourgeoisie is inspired directly by the bourgeoisie itself. Like the Devil who carries the day when he succeeds in persuading us that he doesn't exist, this slippery and transitory class, whose privileges cannot be grounded on air, denies itself in order to affirm itself, convinced that, if it is ever to ensure its earthly rule, it must persuade the ruled of its non-existence. The Nobility, confidently trusting in

---

*Je ris de l'Art, je ris de l'Homme aussi, des chants,
 Des vers, des temples grecs . . .
                    ("Angoisse")
†O Don Quichotte . . . ta vie fût un poème,
 Et les moulins à vent avaient tort, ô mon roi!
                    ("A Don Quichotte")
‡Malraux's quip is appropriate because, in expressing the *paradox* that "life is worth nothing, but nothing is worth life," it strikes at the heart of the problem. His parody, accurately echoing concerns of previous poets, is merely a complacent approval of cowardly thinking.

God, had proudly asserted its privileges; the bourgeoisie whisks them out of sight. The trick is to persuade the oppressed that they have no oppressors. Classes? Come now! Modern society is made up of overlapping social strata, of interpenetrating social layers. One would have to be very clever indeed to say just where the proletariat begins and where it leaves off: it's a purely mental construct. Would you define it in terms of production? Or consumption? Neither definition works. To be sure, there are some stations in life which are more desirable than others, but factors like osmosis, gravitation, symbiosis, etc., increase social mobility and always keep society as a whole well adapted to its functions. This regulative action grants each member of the group a social importance which roughly corresponds to his merits. There is a statistical justice. What do these agitators want? To bring about, in some distant future and by systematic violence, a *classless society*?[87] They must be either liars or lunatics since they don't see, or pretend not to see, that such a society has already been achieved in *our present society*.

The bourgeoisie is not unaware of the fact that it was to fill only a *transitional* role. Since society had become bankrupt, it appointed the élite of the Third Estate as its "receiver," entrusted with the task of liquidating its affairs. But the bourgeoisie refuses to acknowledge the truth about itself. If it did, it would see its own death reflected in the mirror. It remembers but would rather forget that it was originally the class which took on the mission of abolishing the nobility in the name of a classless society. That future society represents at once its ultimate fulfillment and its ruin, its reason for being and its negation. But no one would dare to admit this, since to do so would be tantamount to confessing that the bourgeoisie carries within itself the seeds of its own destruction and that it can fulfill itself only through self-annihilation.

To call a halt to this ineluctable process, it pretends that the operation has already been accomplished, that the liquidation proceedings are over, and that equality has already been attained. Aren't the highest "positions" accessible to everyone? Doesn't the vote of a day-laborer from Quercy count as much as that of a Parisian banker? The bourgeoisie will rid itself of the underlying inequality which its final breakup is meant to bring about by projecting it outside itself in the form of an abstact and atemporal negation. The bourgeoisie *does not exist,* and has never existed. As early as 1791, its formidable analytic power had succeeded in breaking down monarchical institutions. It had no fear of turning this power against itself; and by enacting the Le Chapelier Law,[88] its representatives established for an entire century the individual as the only social reality. "Inasmuch as the abolition of all manner of association among citizens of the same estate or profession is one of the basic foundations of the French constitution, it is henceforth forbidden to reestablish these under any pretext whatsoever. Citizens of the same estate or profession, entrepreneurs, shopkeepers, artisans, and journeymen . . . are moreover forbidden to associate for the purpose of electing presidents, secretaries, or syndics. . . . They are forbidden to promulgate any rules concerning their *purported common interest.* . . . All resolutions and covenants (entered into by citizens of the same profession) shall henceforth be declared unconstitutional and a violation of freedom and of the declaration of the rights of man."

This is how classes are eliminated by a mere stroke of the pen. Trade unions? Collective bargaining? What for? Since there are no common interests! A freely negotiated contract will be the rule and this contract must be negotiated *between individuals.* The common interest of the employers consisted in declaring that they held no common interests. This make-believe suicide on the part of the bourgeoisie was designed to atomize the working class. No intermediate groups should stand between the individual and the State. Society will henceforth *appear* to be no more than a vast multitude of solitary souls. The individual—social atom, residuum of analysis, negative product of self-serving negation—is now an absolute in the real sense of the word, that is to say, an *isolated unit.*

In past centuries, the believer situated man's reality in the fullness of his being, that is, in God, the locus of all affirmations. In contrast to this, the reality of bourgeois man resides in *all that he is not.* The French Revolution created the humanism of non-being. Instead of reintegrating the individual which it had torn away from God into his class, it kept him in a state of isolation and impotence, where his reality was measured only by his possessions. Throughout this period, the bourgeoisie as a *class* operates unnoticed in the background, sometimes concealed by a parliamentary monarchy or a dictatorship, at others by a pseudodemocracy of property owners. It is hardly surprising that popular opinion in the bourgeois era is haunted by the myth of occult powers, Jesuits and Free masons, the Jewish Conspiracy, the Elders of Zion, the wall of money, the conspiracy of munition-makers. These legends naively betray the deepest misgivings of the ordinary citizen. He supposedly enjoys all the rights; yet no sooner does he exercise them than a subtle modification occurs which renders them totally ineffective. He can never recognize his own original intentions in what is presented to him as the product of his actions. The reason is that in bourgeois regimes, whether parliamentary, monarchic, or dictatorial, it is the bourgeoisie as a whole which is the Occult Power.

From the Parnassians to the Symbolists, the poets only glorify the negative self-image that the propertied class wishes to project. To be sure, they are unsparing in their contempt. On close inspection, however, the bourgeoisie they pillory doesn't really exist; or if it does, it consists exclusively of shopkeepers and petty bureaucrats. When in his intimate journal Baudelaire flares up at merchants, when Leconte de Lisle predicts the death of mankind

> . . . on a great heap of gold wallowing in some corner . . .
> You will stupidly die while filling your pockets,*[89]

when Mallarmé rejoices that there are no merchants in his family,[90] or when he describes a bourgeois in his night cap copulating with his frigid wife,[91] their contempt is directed only against small trade. Meanwhile . . . and yet they don't seem to grasp what's going on! About banks, big business, and industry, not a peep. The economic upheavals of their century remain entirely incomprehensible to them, and they confine their sarcasm to a defunct Third Estate. In their writings, the *idea* of the bourgeoisie becomes an atemporal concept. Flaubert rendered an even higher service to his native land. He would define his pet aversion as a quality of the soul: "I call bourgeois everything that thinks basely."[92] A splendid way to add to the confusion! According to such a definition, a

---

* . . . sur un grand tas d'or vautrés dans quelque coin . . .
Vous mourrez bêtement en emplissant vos poches,
("Aux Modernes")

mean-spirited worker will be categorically labeled an honorary bourgeois, while the ever-so-charitable Madame Boucicaut[93] is, thanks to her virtues, exempt from bourgeois status.

About this time, there begins a literary tradition whose principle is to hit hard but off target. Even today, on Parisian stages, a stock bourgeoisie is pilloried to the enthusiastic acclaim of the bourgeois public. As for the noble solitude of the poet, what is it then, if not the reflection of bourgeois separatism? When Baudelaire writes, "Many friends, many gloved handshakes . . ." or "feeling of *loneliness* from childhood,"[94] or when Flaubert compains about "going through unending loneliness to go Lord knows where?",[95] what are they, if not victims of ingenious propaganda? It is not that they *are* isolated, but rather that they *isolate themselves* so that their class may take them as examples of universal solitude. Here is Baudelaire writing about himself: "Universal misunderstanding allows everyone to agree. For if, by some stroke of fortune, people could understand one another, they could never agree. . . . In love, the notion of sharing is the result of a misunderstanding. This misunderstanding is pleasure . . . these two imbeciles are convinced that they think alike. The unbridgeable gulf which creates incommunicability remains unbridged."[96] He is only giving a more tragic and bitter twist to the little phrase in the Le Chapelier Law: "*so-called* interests." Free competition, free trade, the struggle for life: so many bourgeois slogans which are epitomized in Hobbes's aphorism "Homo homini lupus," and which the poets transpose into psychological or metaphysical terms. An all-embracing pessimistic philosophy, which will have no other basis than this, flourishes in the second half of the century. There is scarcely a scribbler or poetaster who won't pretend, with a sigh, to have painfully experienced human impenetrability.

You profound observers, how is it that you fail to notice that what you find in the human heart is only what you have already put there? This incommunicability which you claim to discover in it is nothing less than a principal result of social atomization. If men are indivisible atoms, they could hook onto one another but not interpenetrate. Two substances which have been isolated at the outset could not have any interaction. All of the nasty and bitter psychology which the century handed down to us as the fruit of its experience can be constructed *a priori* once there is a commitment to confront reality by the exclusive use of the analytic method. The only thing left is to *play* at being impenetrable. Everybody is so good at it. It is gratifying to be inscrutable; as for my neighbor's inscrutability, it will serve as an excuse for my not understanding him. Thus words lie; they don't have the same meaning for everyone. Thus love is simply a private turmoil—the object of love having nothing to do with it. "It's not you I loved, but another, born of my dreams." There is no one, not even the poets who assumed an attitude of gentle scorn for woman (that inscrutable companion) who doesn't express, in witty words, the period's misogyny (whose historical, social, and economic reasons are bluntly summarized in Bismarck's motto: *Kinder, Küche, Kirche**).

The evidence? It would be simple but cruel to demonstrate what lurks beneath the subtlest forms of disenchantment. In a rhetorical flourish Lefébure writes that man is too pure for woman.[97] What does he mean? Or rather, how does he *feel* what he says? One of his letters informs us that he hesitates to marry. There are two possible matches, one with a "tall, plain girl," the other with "one who is very pretty and who looks like the Mona Lisa." But the latter shows signs of "a physical passion which terrorized him." Yet she is intelligent and active. No matter. He is thinking instead of marrying the other one: "Cold and drab, apart from her lack of culture, she is perhaps the very woman I need."[98]

These poets have curious illusions. What they refer to as a spiritual aristocracy is in fact the sublimation of bourgeois virtues. But this illusion itself is a creation of the ruling class. It had tried in vain to curb the spirit of analysis; they hoped it would liquidate the appearance of classes and stop there; but this corrosive acid attacks the social atom itself and breaks it down into material atoms. Beset by mortal dread, the bourgeoisie sees the proletariat champion materialism just as, a century earlier, it itself had championed analytic reason. Its most effective weapon now turns against it. I have described how it defends itself by conjuring up a phantom aristocracy: lacking any essence of its own, it will constantly vacillate between the masses to whom it is drawn and the nobility which spurns

*Children, kitchen, church.

it, between the equality it loudly proclaims and the inequality it quietly insinuates, between atheism and Religion for the masses. It recoils in horror from nature because it is nature which makes men equal. Each bourgeois seeks to distinguish himself from common humanity and to tear himself away from the ordinary concerns of everyday life; each one denies his body, suppresses his needs, bases his worth on personal *merits,* and proves by a rigorous asceticism and a worship of the artificial that superior men are above nature. Thus, without realizing it, he transforms himself increasingly into what he already is, and each step forward takes him another step back from the nobility. In contrast, the nobleman, secure in his faith and proud of his birth, is eminently satisfied with nature and unabashedly exhibits his own.

Within this bourgeois Manichean framework the poets transform themselves into pure souls. Their asceticism is the very image of Victorian cant. Never do they resemble the bourgeoisie more closely than when they attempt to set themselves apart from it; for they wish to prove their superiority through denial, through their contempt for life and nature, through negativity; whereas the bourgeoisie, unable to ground its privileges in Being, claims to distinguish itself from the people by means of self-inflicted privations and taboos, that is, through Negations. This *fin de siècle* poetry holds itself up as a mirror in which the ghosts of defunct aristocrats can admire themselves. But what it really reflects, despite itself, is the image of the great industrial and commercial families.

It is true that this image remained unrecognized either by the bourgeoisie or by the poets. How could it have been otherwise, since the bourgeoisie knows that it cannot look upon itself without dying? It shuns its own reflection on principle because it wishes neither to be apprised of what it *is*—which would mean admitting that equality is a lie—nor of what it is *not*—which would embolden the working masses to demand its abolition. For a long time social existence has been nothing more than a form of collective evasion. All controversial subjects are outlawed. Respectable circles had chosen to speak—but only to say nothing. Yet neither the new breed of Gentleman nor the poets can hear the subdued chit-chat of the *salons* in the willful silence of a Poetry which had resolved to speak only to say nothing. During the hypocritical dictatorship of

Napoleon III, the press acts as its own censor, the bourgeoisie remains silent for fear of exposing itself, and the workers are gagged. Meanwhile, the poets make themselves the echo of this silence. And if they persist in looking down on this class whose most singular feelings find expression in their poetry, it is because their very scorn betrays the unconscious disgust they feel for themselves.

Moreover, if they endeavored to bring about the fictitious and radical abolition of the Universe, it was to appease their rancor without compromising themselves. It seemed more comfortable and less dangerous to imagine the sun cooling off[99] than to deal with the social order. Flaubert had taught them the ingenious trick of justifying arbitrary power by using the same arguments that condemn it. We know that this writer, sequestered in Croisset because of his varied occupations, had put his faith in the workers' ability to resist Napoleon. He experienced the delights of disappointment: "For me, 1789 demolished the glory of the nobility, 1848, the bourgeoisie, and 1851 *the people.*"[100] Only one final step remains to be taken: "I am thankful to Badinguet.[101] Let him be praised, for he has restored my scorn for the masses."[102] The argument is foolproof: the poets will extend their contempt for the regime to all of Humanity; but since Humanity itself was contemptible, didn't it have the regime it deserved? Thanks to them, the dictatorship of Napoleon III became its own justification. Without any qualms, Flaubert could visit Napoleon III, receive a decoration, and write, along with countless other gems, the following lines to Princess Mathilde: "The Tuileries Ball lingers on in my memory like something magical, like a dream. I only regret that I could not get close enough to speak to you."[103]

The bourgeoisie never really felt worried. It knew that in times of danger all these silence-strikers would rally to its cause. As a matter of fact, in 1871 Flaubert expressed regrets that "the entire Commune wasn't shipped off to the galleys"[104] and that the "despicable workers"[105] weren't given the punishment they deserved. And the habitually imperturbable Leconte de Lisle, beside himself with rage and fear, shouts: "What a pity that little Moulin still hasn't been shot. Even more disturbing is that in all likelihood that filthy Courbet[106] and his whole despicable gang of painters and etchers won't be lined up in front of a firing squad."[107] How fortunate for the bourgeoisie! It's at crucial moments that you discover who your friends really are.

But, as we have seen, it is the point of view of the lower middle class, even more than that of the ruling élite, which will find expression in their poems. The naturally conservative *petite bourgeoisie* exhibits a rigid attitude of abstract denial; and if you don't wish to define it by its patient and modest work, you then have to seek its essence in its total denial of everything, including its own desires. As the *petit bourgeois* they are, the poets are unwilling to locate their true personal identity in the distinguishing features of their own character. They will choose to see these as nothing more than the abstract affirmation of an empty Ego. This formal and universalistic individualism is diametrically opposed to the operation which the generation of the 1890s will perform on its own sensibility and which they will call the "Cult of the Self."[108] Since they don't like themselves, they can only acknowledge themselves as pure self-negation. Thus they dwell in the realm of the unhappy consciousness, and until 1890 the pure act of negativity constitutes the only intimate connection of self to self. When Marcel Schwob writes that "art stands opposed to general ideas, describes only the universal, desires only the unique . . . ,"[109] he brings the pietism of his predecessors to an end—whereupon literature takes a new turn. Little by little, their Platonism is replaced by the mystique of the pure, ineffable, and indispensable individual, like a "melody" flowing in time. For the present, however, the poets of 1860 do not go beyond their unhappy consciousness. Their transcendental Ego is only an act of negation emptied of content, and their empirical character, which they make no effort to cultivate, remains undeveloped. This dual identity is beneficial to the established moral order. While Mallarmé, "the Prince of the Clouds,"[110] works hard at cultivating "his own pure vision,"[111] his *alter ego,* the compartmentalized and comformist civil servant, attends to his duties and behaves so much like his fellow civil servants that they hardly notice anything special about him. He has no sense of responsibility toward himself. Exercising, a good part of the time, a profession which calls for politeness and the good opinion of others, his principal concern is to reflect a reassuring image of virtue to all the right-thinking people around him, even carrying his elegance to the point of embracing their anti-Semitism. Flaubert and Baudelaire were anti-Semites, Villiers was one and so, alas, was Mallarmé. These hollow civil servants are receptacles for the whole society's prejudices. They are its temporary incarnation. While the poet cries out in scorn against the human race, the humble administrator patiently courts a few honorary distinctions. Flaubert received a decoration, Baudelaire was a candidate for the Académie Française, Leconte de Lisle and Heredia were academicians. They carried this so far that sometimes one wonders if the poet's nihilism wasn't merely an excuse for the functionary's conformism.

But no; these protesters are sincere. It is simply that they mistook their own negativity for an end in itself. They refused to recognize themselves in their social pursuits because these had become anonymous and entirely devoid of meaning. But they didn't realize that these pursuits remained their only *reality*—or else, when they did realize it, they claimed that in their eyes reality didn't count. Throughout this whole time their *humanity*, transcendental and yet empty and ineffectual, had nothing to do with their lives. Unwitting reactionaries, they gave voice to a White Terror, and shared—this being the elegant thing to do—the conservatives' hatred of the human race. During this same period the experimental novel embarked on a different route, headed toward the same goal: the poets bracketed man, while the naturalist novelists scrutinized him with the eye of an entomologist. At issue in both cases is a refusal: in the one case, a refusal to take part in the human enterprise, and in the other, a refusal to accept the values and hopes of this peculiar species of ants which builds its anthills in the open.

What an odd predicament! These martyrs bare their wounds to a heaven they know to be uninhabited, before a crowd which takes no notice of them. At bottom, they have no witnesses other than themselves. "Yes," says a heroine of this age, "it's for myself, for myself alone, that I blossom."[112] They are sincere. The intervention of the Other—when they even consider it—seems to them desirable only insofar as the Other's glance, as it lingers on their poems, leaves a glaze where the poets may see themselves objectively reflected in their works. The greatest and purest among them will later recognize that one of the highest forms of glory for a writer is to see himself brought back to life through the reader's admiration for one of his books.[113] In short, the reader, to the extent that he is tolerated at all, has lost his privileged position as a *supreme end.* He is now a *means;* and this new role assigned to the Public is perhaps one of the most radical metamorphoses undergone by Poetry during this period.

When in former times the artist wrote for the King or for the People, he wouldn't have dreamt of making a show of refinement. He laid his cards on the table. The sweeping effects produced by the great spectacles of Sophocles, Shakespeare, Homer, and Dante were never based on tricks. That's why they are, quite mistakenly, called "natural." But when the bourgeois public ventures into the world of poetry, every trick is permitted. In contrast to the days of the sovereign people, this new public is never offered a straightforward and unadorned work which exerts a *pure compelling force* on any free subjectivity. Now the poets merely seek to *produce an effect*—in just the same way that a young man who considers himself a great lover lightly runs his fingers over a woman's body as if it were a harp and makes the appropriate strings vibrate. This harpist isn't thinking about the woman; if he dreams of making her tremble, it is only to bolster his self-satisfaction. The poet-functionary thinks of the public only as the objectification of his own image. Up to this time, the Word functioned as intermediary between poet and reader. Now it has become a column of silence blossoming alone in some secluded garden; if the reader can scale the walls and catch sight of the fountains, the flowers, and the nude women, he must *from the outset* be made to feel that all of this is not his and has not been put together for his benefit. Someone has arranged a solitary celebration[114] and the indiscreet interloper has stumbled upon some entertainment in progress. Let him admire in silence, then tiptoe out, after being set aquiver by the maddening titillations of Poetry.

In short, the reader now becomes the go-between linking the Poet to the Word. A particular connection has been broken between the Artist and his Public: that of *reciprocity.* In these "solitary celebrations," the penitents of poetry act out their own sacrifice. From time to time they catch sight of a pair of eyes shining at them from behind a hedge, from above the wall and, without letting on that they have noticed anything, they realize with satisfaction that their sacrifice has not been in vain. If these eyes are filled with tears of emotion, so much the better; the poets will only savor their superiority over the masses all the more. Verlaine, for instance—who later would radically change his conception of poetry—declares in the name of the Parnassians and of the young generation of poets that one must "write moving lines very coldly."[115] In short, the great silent sacrifice of the poet requires no witnesses other than accidental ones. The poet *is* his own witness.

Yet the absence of the Other subverts their enterprise. They become actors playing in their own play. It is like performing to a blasé public which knows the dialogue by heart and no longer lets itself be taken in. And at still other moments, they very subtly "take a leap into faith," as Camus would say. Despite all the evidence, despite their own stated intentions, despite atheism, they fall back, tacitly and circuitously, into presupposing the existence of an absolute witness. By dramatizing their personal failure and by pushing it to the point of desperation, they imagined that an absolute consciousness interpreted their defeat as a victory. The all-too-obvious absurdity of Everything, the "sob of the Earth,"[116] their own self-sacrifice and, above all, the agonizing and unshakeable atheism—it is inconceivable that all this could be meaningless.

For someone totally committed to History, losing is unbearable: it is the triumph of the forces of Evil. If he is told that posterity will appreciate his virtues two hundred years hence, he will hardly be impressed. In fact, it couldn't matter less to him. He knows very well that his grand-nephews will no longer be abreast of what was going on, and that they will appreciate his courage and self-abnegation from a quasi-aesthetic perspective since they won't care about the causes which inspired them. For posterity, these causes are but a means, whereas the virtues themselves constitute the end. But for the one suffering defeat, it is precisely the cause which becomes the end and which dictates the means. Would you console Saint-Just with a medal for good conduct while he is standing on the gallows awaiting his turn to die and surveying the ruin of all his work? If, however, you believe in God, failure can, without excessive difficulty, be transformed into victory, since God is both out of the picture—out of *all* pictures—and at the same time our most intimate reality. The Supreme Being, conceived outside of and against history, is totally indifferent to human goals and considers them only as a means. They are mere pretexts to ensure obedience to his law.

The poets we have been discussing reversed the terms: since they do not believe in God, they cannot use their Faith to prove that their life should find its meaning and justification in another world. Yet there is something ineffable and indefinable about their manner, something hinting at the existence of God. It is as if the despair and death of the atheist offers a proof *ad absurdum* of Religion. Once again it is Musset who, in his admirable *Confession of a Child of the Century*, best reveals the workings of this double game: "When an atheist takes out his watch and gives God fifteen minutes to strike him dead, it is clear that he has given himself fifteen minutes of anger and unbearable delight. This was a paroxysm of despair, a great cry of pain, a sweeping appeal to all heavenly powers from a wretched creature trampled underfoot. *And who knows?* In the eyes of *He who sees all,* this was *perhaps a prayer.*"[117]

The grandiloquence of this passage clearly shows that it refers to the heroic period of militant atheism. In pre-Franco Spain, anarchists still hurled such challenges at public meetings; that's because the Spanish god has had a particularly long lease on life. Faith stands in inverse proportion to industrial development. But for the poets of 1860, less easily moved to passion, atheism is not a conquest, but a dreary, inherited certainty. These assiduous unbelievers who go to the limits of disbelief, even draw the absurd conclusion (which is nowhere implied in the premise) that man is mere dust. Their display of zeal in tearing down the image of man is subtle proof that man without a creator is an impossibility. They don't say it; they don't even think it; and yet their dissatisfaction with everything, their conviction that human failure somehow magically implies a victory of man—all this points to an infinite and unnamed presence. As atheists empty of hope, they behave as if the only thing required of them, in this ultimate trial, was to remain steadfast in despair. Around this time just about all intellectuals refuse happiness. Baudelaire writes to Janin: "A man must have fallen very low indeed to believe himself happy."[118] Later on one of his disciples, before he found his own path, will declare in a letter to a friend: "Happiness here on earth is base—one's hands must be calloused indeed to reach for it."[119] But isn't this what a

Christian professes? Even nowadays Monsieur François Mauriac can write in the name of Catholic doctrine: "The worker-priests live in the midst of an atheist working-class, whose hope never rises above the level of earthly things. Though they cannot share the workers' hopes, they can share their sufferings. They are enjoined to testify to the scandalous words: 'My kingdom is not of this world' . . . No, Humanity has no right to hope that an earthly Kingdom where Man has become God will ever appear."

The refusal of happiness during the period when poetry withdraws into itself is all that remains of the Great Hope. When all is said and done, it is an inverted belief in the Kingdom of God. We are all familiar with the despair of the rejected lover: he makes himself more and more depressed until he falls completely to pieces before his silent mistress: "You don't love me as much as I love you. You don't love me anymore. You never loved me. You always hated me." This is because, while refusing to admit it, he knows deep down that he will feel her gentle hand on his brow and hear a soft voice murmur: "I love you." If he were to *believe* what he says, he wouldn't have said it. It is the same thing with our poets. Until their dying day they will live out the dream of the existence of God; and the magic power of their despair will repopulate an Uninhabited Heaven. It's as if, in the all-embracing comedy of the Second Empire, the director had cast them in the role of edifying atheist. In their work as in their life, they give a conscientious portrayal of the misery of man without God. And so it is that a subtle connection—one we shall later have occasion to further in more detail—will be established between the poetry of this period and the Stage. Bad faith, despair experienced as circumstantial evidence of Hope, theatrics and self-reflection: such are the main features of the inner lives of these young men.

But most of them won't see things through to the end; they will give up midway, allowing themselves to trail off into apathy, transitory passions, or whimpering narcissism. Not one of them is capable of holding together, in a single overarching tension, the various and contradictory aspects of their situation and their options. Their dream thus turns into a pipedream. They toy with paradoxes, they cultivate deep personal grudges, they pursue honors, or they enjoy portraying famous moments in history. On occasion they even give up poetry altogether, and the letter announcing the break is not always cordial. Cazalis, later to write under the pseudonym of Jean Lahor, thought that one day he could make a brilliant legal career for himself. Straightaway he writes: "Dream and poetry are two wines which pall after a while, and it wouldn't be such a bad thing if I were to indulge in them a bit less."[120] Others, like Catulle Mendès, will make Poetry itself their career. In short, all the disparate elements which are supposed to be united in poetry are fragmented and experienced in isolation. Because of this, they become stock images, collective representations which derive their experience[121] from a particular historical conjuncture, in short, superstructures which are little more than reflections of the existing social order.

There was no one around who actually experienced the situation poetry was in, no one to internalize these attitudes, mores, and myths. Instead of creating them for himself, each poet borrows them. No one thinks them through; they are accepted because *Other People* are supposed to think them. An anonymous Idea of Poetry, taken up, rejected, then taken up again haphazardly by a bevy of distinguished and pedestrian minds, remains unworthy of itself, more object than idea, a product of inertia and exteriority. If such passive objectivity were to be transcended, someone was needed who could internalize it, impose his personal stamp on it, and live out the Paradox in all its contradictions to the point of dying for it.

If someone could appear for whom the idea of poetry could become a mortal and self-inflicted illness, if an all-embracing lucid consciousness could, in one single act, hold all its nuances together, it would then elude Marxist interpretations and escape social conditioning. If all the errors were stacked up to the limit, they would topple over and reveal the truth of man behind them. Whether such fanciful dreams would testify to the asphyxiation of French thought in the nineteenth century or to the human condition itself would depend on the presence of a volunteer to live them out. The number of poets who frequented the *salons* of Leconte de Lisle and Nina de Villard didn't matter[122]—they were mediocrities. There were certainly no shining lights—at best there were reflectors, but mainly there were fools. All lacked the breadth of vision and the painstaking concern with detail, the rashness and the patience, the mad pride and humility, the obsessive zeal and the lucid intelligence which alone could forge these commonplaces made of soft, spiteful thought into a new and hard alloy. Unable to find its hero and true martyr, poetry's wreath will unravel, its themes will be strewn on the ground and wither and poetry will become what they say it is: an epiphenomenon or, as it was already described by some, a superstructure, a simple and passive product of transformations it knew nothing about, as if it had taken it upon itself to demonstrate by its own example the trenchant and incisive remark that a new Prophet had just made, "Ideas have no history of their own."[123]

# II

## The Chosen One

### 1. A PHANTOM MARRIAGE[124]

The Second Empire nears its end. Every summer, when school lets out, the Poets of Paris note the arrival of a young provincial who teaches English at the Lycée in Tournon, "Short, frail and wasted-looking, with a stern yet mournful face, gentle in its bitterness . . . he* has small, slender hands and the somewhat limp and arrogant gestures of a dandy."† On occasion, he meets with Villiers, Mendès, Coppée, Dierx, and looks up his friend Des Essarts. He was received by Leconte de Lisle and befriended by Banville. Sometimes he opens a little notebook "bound in imitation leather . . . and fastened with a copper clasp"[125] and has them read his poems. Some of these will later be published in the *Parnasse Contemporain*. His decency, his reserve, his modesty, his almost feminine gentleness are disarming. He is well liked, it seems, but not taken too seriously. Mendès, Dierx, Mérat, while appreciating certain of his poems, find him obscure. Leconte de Lisle writes that he is "gentler and crazier than ever, and his prose and poems are completely unintelligible."[126] Coppée notes in his diary that: "I shall surely speak about him again, and at length. This exquisite madman deserves it. But for now I'll simply set down yesterday evening's prize folly." Banville and Coquelin were to put in a good word for his play *The Afternoon of a Faun* at the Comédie Française; but when he

---

*Throughout this section of the text, the "he" Sartre refers to is Mallarmé. Not once here is the poet identified by name.—TRANS.
†Catulle Mendès. Quoted by Mondor, *Vie de Mallarmé*.

gave them the manuscript they were taken aback by a rather long and boring monologue, totally lacking in dramatic action.

Somewhat later, he entertained Catulle Mendès and Villiers in his new home in Avignon. He read them a text so perfectly unintelligible[127] that Mendès could scarcely keep from laughing in his face. Later on, incidentally, Mendès—older and wiser—reproached himself for his reaction and for not having had "the courage to be brutally frank,"[128] which might have saved the soft-headed eccentric and perhaps even transformed him into—who can tell—another Mendès. In short, the young men of the *Parnasse Contemporain*[129] didn't really accept him as one of their own. What was he lacking? A Parisian air, no doubt. Provincial pedantry had stiffened this very sensitive man into a position of unyielding intransigence; moreover, poverty and solitude are not the best counsellors. His elders gently urged him to be sensible. You are right not to compromise, still . . . "You would do more for our cause," Banville writes him, "by arranging your play so that it can be accepted and staged, than by making it more poetic and less stageworthy."[130] In a word, he is an eccentric, whose not very intelligent stubbornness is undermining his real gift. And yet these poets must have recognized in him a perfect image of themselves; they could all see themselves in him since he still remains, at this point, only what the century has made of him. He belongs to the species of poet-bureaucrat. He also seems (with the exception of Glatigny, the drifter) the most poverty-stricken of them all.

In Tournon, despite his good manners, he had from the very start made a bad impression on his job, which convinced the Parisian "albatrosses" that he was one of their own. For unlike Diogenes who proved there is movement by walking, these poets prove they can fly by staggering.[131] His superiors complain about his teaching and scheme to get him transferred elsewhere; his students "heckle him and do imitations of his mannerisms."[132] One could say that the city of Tournon had been singled out to show him, by these petty persecutions, that he was one of the elect; it garlanded him with that crown of thorns known as hard luck, by which the somewhat effete poets of 1865 had replaced the Great Curse that hung over the mighty bards of the Romantic Age.

As for him, gentle and wretched, he lives as decently as he can with his wife and young daughter. He goes about his job without too much effort and suffers conveniently from the prevalent Mid-Century Malaise: "I have so little life that my head droops down on my chest. I drag about like an old man. I am dead, a corpse. The disease of "ideality" doesn't even let me feel the ennui I pray for and dream of. I don't even have the strength to feel ennui."[133]

These declarations ought to speak in his favor; but no—they are a bit disquieting. Of course these gentlemen of the *Parnasse Contemporain* devote themselves to scorning everything, but not without treating themselves with a certain indulgence, if only to help them survive. The road is long and has just begun, so they indulge themselves. But this young madman doesn't dream of sparing himself. He will drop from exhaustion a few yards from the starting line. His provincial background doesn't allow him to relish the grains of Attic salt which his fellow poets add to their excommunications. He takes everything literally. His condemnations are the least strident of them all, but he believes in them without reservation and strictly molds his life according to his principles. He is a suspicious character.

Is there nothing for him in this world? Nothing at all. He loathes his profession: "Like a stupid circus horse I run around in a narrow circle to the tune of God knows what music! Good Lord! . . . Each day discouragement overwhelms me. I'm dying of tedium. I'll wind up completely wiped out, a wreck."[134]

And his wife? Does he at least love her? No. This young German governess at first pleased him because she was "distinguished looking, sad."[135] In brief, she fulfilled the requirements of both Baudelairian poetry and contemporary bourgeois standards; Baudelaire's description of Madame de Cosmelly fits her well: "She seemed to seek out abandoned places and would sit down with sadness . . . sometimes distractedly holding a book she didn't read."* No doubt she too could sometimes be seen with "her head gracefully drooping towards the flowerbeds in an attitude of almost studied melancholy."† The future teacher, at this time an employee in the Re-

---

*Baudelaire, "La Fanfarlo" [*Oeuvres complètes*, 530].
†Baudelaire, "La Fanfarlo" [*Oeuvres complètes*, 532].

corder's Office, didn't have to look any further: "On her face she wore that trace of lonely grief which was enough for us. We asked for nothing more."[136]

Nothing more, indeed! Why bother finding out whether this grief is feigned or real, passing or constant? What counts is that she provided the Poet with an outward image of his own grief. From the very day he met her he saw in her his own reflection. She was in exile in France just as he was an exile on earth. Moreover, "she is sad and bored here, and I'm sad and bored too. Perhaps from the melancholy we both share, we might create some happiness."[137] The truth is that at first he didn't dream of marrying her. He seduced her rather coldly, perhaps to persuade himself that he was Valmont or Samuel Cramer,[138] or perhaps he wanted to play Hamlet and she was his Ophelia. In London, amid endless quarrels, he did seem to care for her a bit, but later, when he was really sure he no longer loved her, he married her out of obligation and remorse; also, perhaps, not to miss this splendid opportunity to ruin his life.

Now there she is beside him, embroidering and darning and already pregnant. Of course she embodies in her frail and solitary person all the real and ideal wives—especially ideal—of these Gentlemen. So much so that her exact description can be found in their works, particularly in the lines the bachelor Verlaine, who had never laid eyes on her, wrote at this time. She is:

> Gentle, thoughtful . . . and never surprised,
> And sometimes kisses your brow, like a child!*[139]
> ("Wish")

She certainly has

> . . . a sister's quiet abandon.†[140]
> ("Lassitude")

---

*Douce, pensive . . . et jamais étonnée,
 Et parfois vous baise au front, comme un enfant!
                    ("Voeu")
†. . . l'abandon paisible de la soeur.
         ("Lassitude")

And her far-off voice, grave yet so calm,
Speaks in tones of cherished voices which are stilled.*[141]

("My Familiar Dream")

Her husband could hardly improve on the collective portrait of these Pre-Raphaelites. It seems as if the young woman has "an olden look." But we already knew that: we can see, in this faded, "antique" light, born of two dead stars, the visual transposition of "the tones of cherished voices which are stilled." And we guessed it, didn't we? That she had no taste for action, hated new things, loved "the grace of faded objects."[142] In short, there is something about her—was it discretion or a lack of vitality—which makes us not notice her *presence* or confuse it with a phantom of our memory. What a virtue for a bourgeois wife, this slight uncertainty of being! You can never be sure without close inspection whether she really *is* in the room or whether she *had been* there. With exceptional self-abnegation, Marie Gerhard follows the example of those quietists who, to remove themselves from life and from Being, sought to create a permanent confusion of past and present so they could view their perceptions as if they arose from the depths of their memory. No matter. No married couple was ever more monstrously suited for one another. He is a substitute teacher and she is a governess. He is a civil servant and the son of a civil servant; the father of the bride is a government employee.

Naturally, like Verlaine, Corbière,† and so many others, he adopts the idiom in vogue since the time of Baudelaire. Marie is his sister, the "gentle sister" of his letters, the "calm sister" of his poems. Refined love willingly adorns itself with the feathers of incest. If we absolutely must sleep with a woman, then for God's sake, let it be with our sisters. They will lend some spice to the unspeakable insipidness of natural love. And even though we shall have succumbed to Nature, it is in the long run Nature itself that we shall

---

*Et pour sa voix, lointaine, et calme, et grave, elle a
L'inflexion des voix chères qui se sont tues.

("Mon Rêve Familier")

†Cf., for example, "Steam Boat":

My sister for a day / My sister for love-play.

[Ma soeur d'un jour / Ma soeur d'amour.]

have profaned. Besides, by this simple act of labeling, we shall replace vulgar promiscuity with a despondent union at once sad, perverse, and refined. Moreover, the word will stealthily undermine the extravagant temperament of these young women. Perhaps it will dampen their ardor and perhaps the fear of incest will keep them from falling too often into temptation. In time, they might even learn to be satisfied with a few passing frolics. These young men sometimes sing the praises of love but are not keen on making it. To an overeager girlfriend Verlaine suddenly reveals the blood tie that unites them: My sister! Straightaway he takes advantage of her astonishment to propose that they call off their lovemaking. Couldn't they replace it with tears?

> Place your brow on my brow and your hand in my hand . . .
> And let us weep till dawn, my wanton child!*[143]
>
> ("Lassitude")

Tormented by his own frightening sexuality, Baudelaire exalted the cold majesty of frigid women. His more sedate epigones adopt his misogyny and his myths. But this misogyny is that of the surrounding bourgeoisie, and what they aim for is not some fearsome whirlwind of pleasure where sadism and masochism intermix; it is domestic tranquillity. Seminal emissions upset them. Won't too frequent ejaculations produce a waste of brainmatter? Later on Mirbeau[144] will echo their fears which Porto-Riche, in *Amoureuse*, will accentuate. This era resounds with the grievances of harassed males. Did women make so many demands? I find that hard to believe. Our grandmothers and mothers knew the price of frigidity. I am inclined to believe that these refined and perverse bourgeois were lacking in passion. In fact this English teacher, unhappy with his poetry, attributes his poetic impotence to a "youthful priapism" whose subsequent manifestations one would be hard put to detect. For this materialist, the sexual act is condemned by some shadowy verdict. He made sure not to awaken the soft, cold flesh of his wife.

---

*Mets ton front sur mon front et ta main dans ma main . . .
  Et pleurons jusqu'au jour, ô petite fougueuse!

  ("Lassitude")

A society based on incest, Durkheim once said, would be unspeakably dreary. Conjugal relations, subjected to rigid imperatives, would hardly be distinguishable from other kinship ties. By transforming his wife into a sister, the young husband cunningly refashioned her into a domestic angel. He thus metamorphosed their carnal relationship into a blood tie. Sooner or later, of course, incest creeps into households. As Leiris[145] put it so well (I quote from memory): you begin by sleeping with the woman you love and you wind up making love to the mother of your children. Yet no one, up to the end of the last century, thought of *starting off* with the incest.

Besides, what was this odd companionship really about? Avoiding reciprocity. In the thirteenth century, monks had displayed a fear-stricken hatred of the opposite sex. Their misogyny was a direct result of priestly celibacy—a form of propaganda, a defense mechanism, resentment. The old monastic misogyny was revived by the new secular priesthood, who steeped themselves in it for the very same reasons. How could they dream of establishing a household on an equal footing? Woman is natural, therefore abominable. The label "sister," bestowed only on wives, is obviously a purification ritual. You save them from fearsome Nature by imposing virtues on them which are the very negation of feminine instincts. A poet's wife—frigid, devoted, quiet, self-effacing—is the negation of woman, just as a poet is the negation of man. As a result she is no longer anything other than her husband's watered-down counterpart. Verlaine had asked his sister to love and understand him. He had hoped "that his heart, transparent to her eyes alone, might cease to be a problem."[146] The teacher from Tournon has more modest expectations. Understanding supposes still too much initiative: let her be content with reflecting him. He writes that "it is not with precepts that an artist's soul is forged. It must be kindled gently and continuously. If the woman you have chosen is only an artist thanks to her literature teacher, she is a blue-stocking . . . if she is a serious artist in her own right, only the kisses of her beloved can make her blossom. After two years with me, Maria will be my reflection."[147]

Two years have elapsed and he repeats—now with a trace of

melancholy: "She is my angelic and heavenly shadow, but her sweet nature could not transform her into my Lady Macbeth."[148] He reads her his poems; later on she will confess that she doesn't understand them at all. He knows it, yet reads them anyway. Sometimes he sheds tears of anguish before her and when he does, she stares at him silently, fear-stricken and uncomprehending. Little by little, he starts speaking about her in a different tone. She takes on a double identity. For all others she is *the wife* of a civil servant, and he insists that she be treated with respect. His closest friend, his "brother" and "initiator,"[149] one day takes the liberty of showing up with an "illicit companion." The poet considers his wife compromised and will have nothing more to do with such an ill-mannered friend. But, in private, he makes her progressively younger, and by replacing the fraternal bond with a paternal one, he turns her into his daughter's twin sister. Here he is, after several months of marriage, already filled with fatherly indulgence: "Marie, my little German girl, went out for a minute and left her mended stockings on my copy of Baudelaire. I am so amused by it that I cannot disturb them."[150] And, three years later, speaking of his wife and daughter, he describes them as "two little women who quarrel, constantly sulk and gossip from the moment I enter the room."[151] Indeed, for a few decades, the cult of the child-woman, imported from England, where Lewis Carroll and Dickens cultivate suspect desires for little girls, will become established in France and replace the cult of the sister.

But our young civil servant has no special tenderness for child-women. He has a wife and that is all. One is supposed to have a wife. When they were still young and foolish, she was a sister; now she is "Madame." Docile and somewhat miserable, she will be a good housekeeper throughout her life. She was only a flickering light in the thick Germanic shadows; would he have married her if not for that? He almost succeeded in snuffing out this light; the death of her second child would do the rest. After that no one will take notice of her. Betrayed, suffering, a bit whiny, and somewhat of a nag, tyrannizing her daughter in a spirit of revenge, she will subsequently be seen at an occasional concert. A most subtle and criminal stratagem succeeded, without violence, in murdering this woman. Without ever giving her cause to complain, this sweet and very charming husband completely robbed her of her flesh and spirit. Only a shadow lingered on. But that is what best suited the poet: a phantom wife eaten away by abstractions and regrets, who inspired in him only abstract feelings.

Certainly he loved his daughter—but only later—when she goes with him to the theater, to call on his friends, or when she serves punch to his Tuesday visitors, and he is ever so proud of her. In 1864, he welcomes her birth without the slightest show of enthusiasm. Of course, old grandmother Desmolins will say that he is "crazy about her"; but that was only the appropriate thing to say. After managing to utter a few conventional words, he lets his friends see his disenchantment. He is very happy—that goes without saying—but his happiness fails to bring him to life. And he goes on to say that "life's events appear too insubstantial for me to take pleasure in them."[152] Several days later he tells Aubanel: "This crying, naughty baby drove Hérodiade[153] away." When his baby is being nursed, he contemplates it resentfully. "Geneviève, who eats her mother, of course is blossoming like a rose, but my poor Marie, who is being eaten, is pale and forever worn out."[154] He takes some of this back, of course, and writes Cazalis: "My daughter is so beautiful." But his pity for this angelic reflection of himself is really meant for him: he is the one who is being eaten. This voracious child is killing him. "It is cold, so pitifully cold, that I remain huddled in a corner next to Marie's stove which is going full blast for the baby's sake. I get home, worn out from teaching class which robs me of almost all my time and Geneviève never stops getting on my nerves with her crying."[155]

He had friends, of course. Especially two: Cazalis and Lefébure. Later there will be Villiers, Coppée; Glatigny will come to call on him. He writes long answers to their long letters. Could it be said that he likes them? With his mind, yes. But not with his heart. One day he writes: "The heart? I don't know what that means. The brain? With it I relish my art and at one time even enjoyed the company of a few friends."[156] But it is still better if they are not present: "It is really only after my friends have left that I start being with them, with their memory so close to a dream which is sometimes disturbed by their actual presence."[157] Moreover, he stops writing them because he feels a need for an "unknown silence."[158]

He breaks off with Lefébure over a matter of propriety without a trace of regret. Slowly Cazalis will drift away from him without his lifting a finger to stop it; one might think he never even noticed. On the other hand, he was always happy to meet Villiers; they talk and hardly need words to understand one another. Then they separate for months—sometimes years of silence go by before they meet again.

Will nature help him get outside himself? Later, he will say that it gave his youth a fervor "which I call passion."[159] But only as a *spectacle*, as something to be observed at a distance. To understand *his* way of loving nature, we must take away the unspoiled, impenetrable qualities *we* attribute to it. For us, nature reveals unadorned life and pure Being. It establishes the sharp outer fringes of thought. In it we love each blade of grass which, unlike a nut or bolt, could just as easily sprout up elsewhere; we not only love its leaves, of which no two are ever alike, but also its ever sweet and absurd luxuriance. Nature brings out our mimetic tendencies; and instead of projecting our "inner states" onto it, we try to experience the qualities of grass and water. We would like nature to touch and envelop us and, in intimate embrace, to fill us with its blind principles. At bottom, we are asking it to lend a renewed richness to our lives.

The poet of Tournon, however, does not *touch* either stone or plant. Nature, for him, is never something to be felt, something in which he might participate, but merely something to be seen; his gaze keeps it at a distance. He calls it "a tangible Idea."[160] Most of us look to nature for pure individuality—or at least some vague individualizing quality. But he, along with most of the poets of his age, sought generality and repetition. From his window he could observe the yearly and daily renewal of celestial ceremonies. But since it was he who ordained them, he ran no risk of being startled by their course or of learning from them anything whatsoever. Yet is he really the one who ordained them? Was it not rather a vague and lazy poetic way of thinking? Here is exactly what he wrote:

> My favorite season of the year is made up of those last languishing days of summer which come just before autumn, and my favorite time of day is the hour of my evening walk

when the sun comes to rest just before it vanishes. Similarly, my favorite literature is the decadent poetry of the last days of Rome.[161]

He thinks he can account for his tastes; since his sister's death, "strangely and oddly enough," he liked all that could be summed up in the word "fall."[162] Yet already by 1861 Verlaine, who had no sister, was writing:

> The autumn and the setting sun! Oh happiness!
> Blood upon the rot.*

> A fire at the zenith! Death in nature! . . .
> How I love you, bitter autumn, preferred season . . .†[163]

And a little later:

> . . . poison
> Drowns my senses, soul and reason,
> And mingles in a mighty swoon
> Memory with Dusk.‡[164]

Undoubtedly, love for autumn and evening is an "idea collectively shared," an imperative for the poetic sensibility around 1865. The meditation on autumn is one of those spiritual exercises which

---

*L'automne et le soleil couchant! Je suis heureux!
Du sang sur de la pourriture!

Baudelaire's verse comes to mind: "The sun drowned in its own clotted blood." ["Le soleil s'est noyé dans son sang qui se fige."] Surely Baudelaire also liked the fall; he "loves it and praises it" ("Brumes et Pluies"). But one could not say that he had a special predilection for that season. The love of autumn alone becomes a commonplace for the next generation.

†L'incendie au zénith! La mort dans la nature! . . .
Moi, je t'aime, âpre automne, et te préfère . . .
                    ("Un soir d'octobre")

‡                    . . . le poison
Noyant mes sens, mon âme et ma raison,
Mêle dans une immense pâmoison
Le Souvenir avec le Crépuscule.
                    ("Crépuscule du Soir Mystique")

members of the brotherhood annually imposed upon themselves—just as the evening prayer is a daily uplifting. And surely the poet of Tournon is right to see in sunset, in the death throes of summer, symbols of that human tragedy, the fall. But it is not his sister's passing that the celestial death throes reflected back to him; this dead young woman is also merely a symbol. What the poet reads in Nature is the decadence of poetry, the imminent death of Man, the final empyrosis: in a word, the fears of the bourgeois intelligentsia. We cannot count on the spectacles of Nature to dispel our dismal sterility, distress, and doubts.

Exile, Ideal, Dissatisfaction, Contempt: commonplaces that express the pampered sullenness of poets. Neither more nor less than his Parisian friends, the poet-teacher prefers autumn to spring, dusk to dawn, decadence to taking wing. Like all of them, he finds man "too pure for woman." With them, he shares this "delicate, exotic, alien soul . . . always in a state of nostalgia . . ."[165] Why is it, then, that his fellow poets don't quite accept him as one of their own?

Because he ventured to *live* according to their principles. Instead of playing with the distinguished—the ever so distinguished—feelings of the poets, one might say that he became a prey to them, that he was devoured by them. He is not content to taste the decadence so dear to these scornful souls—he embodies it; he symbolizes it through his own decadence; he makes himself into an "old man . . . wiped out . . . a wreck." Leconte de Lisle had made it clear that Parnassian imperturbability was merely a front. Why, then, did this young civil servant feel the need to *make* himself imperturbable? And why should he stretch the esoteric smiles of his friends into an open disdain for the public?

To the disconcerted Parisian poets, the young provincial seems both their caricature and their victim. He takes everything at face value: nobody had asked that much of him. And anyway, where will it all get him? His only love, Poetry, seems to desert him. As soon as he is alone, at the very first chance, he throws himself into his writing like a "desperate maniac."[166] But nothing comes. Or hardly anything. Strictly speaking, this impotence is characteristic of the period—but the other poets manage to adjust to it. He, however, suffers from it, despairs of it. He cries to anyone who will listen: "I'll never be anything but an amateur,"[167] or else, "I'm through as a poet."[168] We are tempted to say that the negative poetry of the Second Empire had chosen this extremist as its agent—to bring about its solemn suicide. To protect themselves from the spell cast by their too perfect recollection, these despairing nihilist poets are driven to preach the very virtues they previously denounced: a sound realism, good sense, opportunism. In brief, the mere existence of this provincial civil servant compels the Parisian poets to question their authenticity and the extent of their belief in the Dream. How does this come about? And who is he anyway?

## 2. THE DEAD HAND OF THE PAST

It would be hard to imagine a better victim. One might say he was made to order: "Ever since the Revolution, both my maternal and paternal families made up an uninterrupted line of functionaries in the Recorder's Office."[169] One day they were destined to unite. And in fact, on 14 June 1841, through the agency of his own daughter Elisabeth-Félicie, the Director of the Office of Records and Deeds "married" his assistant director. In the four days that followed a child was conceived.*[170] What an admirable conjunction of age, sex, and office: through the marriage of his daughter Elisabeth, the superior was beholden to his underling; but as Director and father-in-law, he reestablished his authority. By this summer marriage, the Recorder's Office became its own wife; it loved itself and knew itself biblically. This self-fertilization process was destined to give birth to the Functionary-in-itself, admirable distillation of two lines of functionaries.† If it is true that the Idumaeans reproduce without women, here we have the real "child of an

*Stéphane Mallarmé, born on 18 March 1842.—ED.
†The translator disclaims responsibility for this account of Mallarmé's lineage, in which some may find that Sartre's idiosyncratic humor is exercised at the expense of clarity.—TRANS.

Idumaean night."[171] He would later write—and we readily believe him—that "the career for which I was destined from the cradle"[172] was in the Recorder's Office.

According to explorers and missionaries, there are some savages foolish enough to believe that their progeny are the dead come back to life. Eskimos name their newborn children after recently deceased kin, and Kingsley informs us that certain black Africans place within a baby's reach objects which had previously belonged to someone who had just died. If the infant reaches for it, everyone exclaims: "Look! Grandfather recognized his pipe."

I never read this without smiling. Why tell us about Eskimos or Africans when these customs are in fact our own! And what are our children if not the dead come back to life? Most of the time it is the father, already dead of rancor and gall, who recognizes himself as reemerging from his mother's womb with one more chance. But it could also be an uncle. Or an abstract idea, a principle, a virtue, or a role. Anyway, the child will never be *himself as a separate person.* His parents' solicitude will teach him to feel like an incarnation or a replica, in short, someone Other than himself. From this standpoint, it is the Idumaean child who fares best: he can simultaneously embody all his ancestors since they are all alike.

> Frigid roses all destined to live
> Alike . . .*[173]

created this rosebud. There is only one life for the whole family, and it is handed down from generation to generation. The destiny of the newborn child is so entirely prearranged that it is no longer clear whether a birth or a death is being commemorated. But so many bureaucratic guardian angels were watching over this cradle that great expectations were in order. One day they will observe the emergence of a fastidious little bug, nimble, fully formed, and ready to propagate the species.

Suddenly something cracks: the virgin who had served as go-between, considering her function accomplished, bows out. Who was she? Much later, her mother would deplore "the lively imagina-

---

*De frigides roses pour vivre
  Toutes la même . . .

tion which so thoroughly wore her out."* These words hint at a well-bred murder or an induced suicide. It's bad enough to be born into the Recorder's Office—but then to marry into it as well! Elisabeth-Félicie registers the politest and the clearest protest imaginable: she bequeathes two children to the Recorder's Office—an administrator and a future wife of an assistant director—then, after a trip to Italy, she dies. That the true meaning of this death did not pass unnoticed by the Administration is suggested by the letter I just quoted. It also seems as if the assistant director's remarriage was a vaguely disturbing sign. Even though it took place four years after Elisabeth's death, the remarriage was frowned upon in the Recorder's Office; the period of mourning seemed unduly brief. (Life went on more slowly in the civil service.) And besides, on this occasion, the widower was marrying into business. And even if both sides of the family failed to grasp Elisabeth-Félicie's despair, we can be sure that the child harbored no illusions about it.

Did the loss of his mother have an immediate and decisive impact on him? We have no idea. We possess only one piece of information, and its source is doubtful: "Several days after the event, his grandmother received a visitor in the living room and, as the person spoke about the recent misfortune, the child, embarrassed about his failure to show grief with an appropriately mournful demeanor, decided to roll on the carpet, with his long hair thrashing about his temples."†

Assuming this story to be true, I am not too sure what we can conclude from it. The heart has its shifting moods. Above all, however, the distress of children is incommensurate with the conventional means of expressing it which we place at their disposal. In our adult world, we have turned grief into an atmospheric disturbance generating recurrent storms; it is maintained and drawn out by ritual dances and sartorial ceremonies. For the child, grief can be anything at all. A child whose mother is leaving on a long trip offhandedly accepts her goodbye kiss and goes on with his games. The next day he will *catch* the measles. The measles are his distress. Some other child, normally cheerful, will take to lying, stealing, or bed-wetting when his parents get a divorce. It is wrong for us to say that they do not

*Cf. Mondor, *Vie de Mallarmé*.
†Mondor, *Vie de Mallarmé*, 13. This anecdote was related by Henri de Régnier, who claimed he heard it directly from Mallarmé.

know how to suffer; it is rather that we have turned suffering into a polite little social round and have substituted loud and harmless lamentations for the frightening disorientation it provokes.

A better question might be whether this death was at the origin of a deep trauma in the life of the young boy. Did he feel later on in life that he had been transformed by it? We know what the "verdant paradise of childhood loves"[174] meant to Baudelaire. Crépet[175] quotes a note by Buisson[176] which allows us to understand his well-known "fracture": "Baudelaire was a very delicate soul . . . who was fractured at the first impact of life." Baudelaire could never reconcile himself to his mother's second marriage. But the young orphan we have been speaking about later became the most secretive of men. Allusions to a lost Paradise in his works are few and far between:

> When you see my eyes wandering off in paradise
> I recall bygone years when I drank your milk.*
>
> <div align="right">(<i>Hérodiade</i>)</div>

> A glory for which I once fled—adorable
> Childhood with its woods of roses under nature's Azure . . .†
>
> ("Weary of the bitter rest . . .")

> . . . the fairy with her cap of brightness
> Who once passed over the peaceful sleep of her pampered child,
> Ever letting fall from her unclenched hands
> Snow-white bouquets of fragrant stars.‡
>
> ("Apparition")

I would not say that these lines express genuine regret. Since the time of Baudelaire, lost childhood had been a favorite theme of

---

*Si tu me vois les yeux perdus au paradis,
  C'est quand je me souviens de ton lait bu jadis.
†Une gloire pour qui jadis j'ai fui l'enfance
  Adorable des bois de roses sous l'azur
  Naturel . . .
                    ("Las de l'amer repos . . .")
‡. . . la fée au chapeau de clarté
  Qui jadis sur mes beaux sommeils d'enfant gâté
  Passait, laissant toujours de ses mains mal fermées
  Neiger de blancs bouquets d'étoiles parfumées.

poetry. How are we to know whether the nostalgia for childhood inspired the feeling of exile, or whether, on the contrary, the feeling of exile found its poetic expression in the nostalgia for childhood? Some critics have tried to show that "his mother's death, then his sister's, constituted a great and painful shock to his sexual make-up."[177] I must say that I'm not convinced. The poetic themes of the Idumaean child were not exclusive to him. They were shared by his entire generation. The "great tide of other-worldly love,"[178] the incestuous eroticism, the taste for failure and for Non-Being, the desperate idealism, the Manicheanism, the preciosity, the nihilism: these various themes pervaded the *objective spirit* of the period, and all of them express the historical and social connection as much, if not more than, the history of a particular individual. We can find them as far back as Verlaine's early poetry and his *Poèmes saturniens*.[179] Yes, I know that Verlaine abandoned them to follow his own path, whereas our poet experienced them profoundly and impressed his own indelible stamp on them. Yet the fact remains that he did not invent them, but chose them.

The real problem is this: should an interpretation be based on collective history or on the history of a single individual? On what is called the "dialectical materialist method" or on psychoanalysis? When M. Mauron writes that every poem "contains a hell fashioned in 'the likeness of man' and that it can be deciphered like a dream without taking its poetic and common meaning into account,"[180] we readily agree.*

---

*With the following reservation, however: the poetic themes in the case at hand were borrowed. If the poet appropriated them, it was *by working on them* over a period of thirty years of active deliberation which gradually impregnated them with new meanings. If in spite of this they still manage to betray his secret, it is not because they reveal the nature of his veiled sexual history or of his raw instincts.

Chiseled, polished, and consciously bent into shape, these themes should not be plumbed for mysterious insights they do not possess. If we do grant that they are able to disclose mysterious secrets, they would reveal what I would call "a mystery unbared," "the shadowy side of lucidity."

There is, indeed, an unconscious lodged in the heart of consciousness. This is not some obscure power, for we know full well that consciousness is consciousness through and through; it is introjected finiteness. Mallarmé was deeply tormented by things we understand *today* but which were beyond his ken in his own time.

Our aim is to comprehend his images (gaps in his knowledge, biases, unjustified choices, etc.)—in short, the negative features of the poet, rather than the positive characteristics he unwittingly possessed. What he then considered normal or self-evident or natural is no longer so for us now.

But what does this deciphering give us? "The symbolic expression of an unconscious together with its complexes," is M. Mauron's reply.[181] Why *that* and *only* that? The "active ideologists," Marx tells us, "are specialists in forging the ruling class's illusions about itself."[182] Most of them, of course, are sincere—hence mystified. The shipwreck in *A Throw of the Dice* very accurately reflects the terror of the propertied class, which is becoming aware of its inevitable decline, the malaise of the bourgeoisie confronted with the death of God, the cultivation of decadence by contemporary ideologists, and the sullenness of the man filled with resentment, along with his will to failure. It might also be, as M. Mauron would have it, that this shipwreck represents "criticism of the father and self-criticism*—along with a fulfillment of desire, since in any event the sea and death emerge triumphant." But this would be a case of *overdetermination*, since the same symbol refers us back to two distinct orders of symbolized things. It is claimed that *A Throw of the Dice* is an "Oedipal" poem because "the sea is one of the most frequent symbols for the mother." I will go along with that. But I should also point out that the theme of the sea is inspired by Baudelaire, and I readily believe that *in Baudelaire* it is of Oedipal origin. Yet *for that very reason* I am not sure that it retains this value in the works of his imitators. Besides, in the case of our author, I don't think that we are dealing with an "archetypal" theme, one whose existence seems to reach back into time immemorial. In 1859 he speaks of

. . . the dark rock
Which loomed up like a giant and was nibbled by the waves.†[183]
("Her Grave Is Dug! . . .")

---

*At this point, however, Mauron begins to go astray. Mallarmé's self-criticism (not at issue here) is *most certainly* conscious and deliberate, as is shown by *Igitur,* where it already appears. Why, then, place it on the same level as the unconscious critique of the father?

†. . . rocher sombre
Qui, géant, se dressait, et qu'a rongé le flot.
("Sa Fosse est Creusée! . . .")

and calls England an

> old rock battered by the foam.*[184]
> ("Her Grave Is Sealed")

We can, if we wish, see these words as a prefiguration of:

> ... *a rock*
>
> *false manor*
>   *at once*
>     *evaporated into mist*
>
>   *which set*
>     *a boundary on the infinite.†*
>     *(A Throw of the Dice)*

   But the least that can be said is that we do not have to see things this way. Thereafter, no future mention of the sea appears until "Sea Breeze" ("Brise Marine," May 1865). In 1869, *Igitur* establishes the indissoluble connection between "the complexity of the sea and the stars,"[185] and we know from Coppée's account that the broad outlines of his symbolic cosmology were already blocked out by 1872. But the theme of the Ocean does not undergo any noteworthy development prior to 1873. Of course, he does write from Tournon that he cannot write a poem without some "aquatic fantasy"[186] seeping into it. But here, the function of water seems to be exclusively that of a mirror. It is always stagnant waters, an untroubled stream, lake, or pool; it hardens or liquifies as required. It appears most likely that it was the ever-increasing obsession with the Shipwreck which broke down the notion of liquidity so as to

*vieux roc que bat l'écume.
("Sa Fosse est Fermée, July 1859)
†     ... *un roc*

*faux manoir*
   *tout de suite*
     *évaporé en brumes*

   *qui imposa*
     *une borne à l'infini.*
   *(Un Coup de Dés, May 1879)*

recast it in a new set of symbolic functions. In his final years,* this concept will embody the infinite disorder of matter and the reign of Chance—in other words, the misery of man without God, the *collective* theme of the epoch.† It therefore appears that the aquatic fantasy underwent a transformation under the influence of *adult* preoccupations and that the process of transformation was entirely conscious. When the young poet's narcissism yielded to the tragic conception of the hero, the pure realm of reflection became an inhuman external power. Can a symbol which has been so self-consciously refashioned still retain its obscure dimension? Yes, up to a point. But it is obvious that the psychoanalytic method cannot be applied without modification.

The real enigma to be solved here is more complex. How can we use two methods which claim to be mutually exclusive? How can a

---

*"Salutation" ("Salut"); "To the Sole Care of Voyaging" ("Au seul souci de voyager"); "To the Overwhelming Cloud" ("A la nue accablante"); *A Throw of the Dice* (*Un Coup de Dés*).
†Compare:
  Verlaine:

> Weary of life and in dread of dying, like
> A brig adrift, a plaything of the ebb and flow,
> My soul sets sail for frightful shipwrecks.
> > ("Anguish": *Poèmes saturniens*)

> Lasse de vivre, ayant peur de mourir, pareille
> Au brick perdu jouet du flux et du reflux,
> Mon âme pour d'affreux naufrages appareille.

["Angoisse," *Poèmes Saturniens*. Final printing October 1866.]

  Mallarmé:
> The flesh is sad, alas! . . .
> To fly far away! . . .
> . . . . . . . . . . . . . . . . . . . . . . . . . . . . . . . . . . . . . . . . . . . . . . . . . . . . . . .
> And perhaps the masts, inviting storms,
> Are of those which a wind bends over shipwrecks
> Lost, without masts, without masts or fertile isles . . .
> > ("Sea Breeze")

> La chair est triste, hélas! . . .
> Fuir! là-bas fuir! . . .
> . . . . . . . . . . . . . . . . . . . . . . . . . . . . . . . . . . . . . . . . . . . . . . . . . . . . . . .
> Et, peut-être, les mâts, invitant les orages
> Sont-ils de ceux qu'un vent penche sur les naufrages
> Perdus, sans mâts, sans mâts, ni fertiles îlots . . .

["Brise Marine": Tournon, 1865. In *Parnasse Contemporain*, May 1866.]

single thematic ensemble symbolize a personal and sexual destiny and at the same time a moment in social history? And if it were determined that both these systems should simultaneously be taken into account, what relationship should we establish between these two orders of meaning? Interpretation, absolute separation, one-way influence of one upon the other, reciprocal interaction? If we have chosen the case of the "Obscure Sphinx"[187] of Tournon, it is because it seemed to provide us with the privileged opportunity to confront, in a concrete case, the psychoanalytic and Marxist methods of interpretation.

A clever fellow who, with downcast eyes, acknowledges: "I know that I know nothing" might conceivably be Socrates. An imbecile who puts on a conceited air and says "I don't know" is a positivist. With what morose pleasure did the Gentlemen of 1920 prophesy the Great Penance. The positivist resembles them: he prescribes the limits of human knowledge with the cheerful resignation of the middle classes. Thanks to him, ignorance becomes something distinguished. As an inconsolable atheist, he avenges the Death of God by prophesying the Great Penance of the Mind. Psychoanalysis pays its homage to positivism, which has always pretended to ignore the difference between empiricism and objectivity. It strives to be an empirical discipline, to situate the patient's experience within the world, and gradually to bring to light his empirical relations to his environment. These relations and even their investigation presuppose a prior condition—namely that the patient, the objects affecting him, and the psychoanalyst himself all belong to the same ontological system.

For the psychoanalyst, that goes without saying. He encounters a collection of concomitant facts and studies their reciprocal relationships. Why should he question the *possibility* of their being given together since it is *precisely together* that they are given to him? According to him, the relations he uncovers (cause and effect, means and ends, history and character, taboo and violation of taboo, sexual instinct and death instinct, libido and censorship, etc.) are based on an ontological link of pure contiguity, or, if one likes, on simple proximity. But this link is both *contingent* (the *fact is* that a particular man had particular parents and a particular childhood) and *external;* the terms reciprocally modify one another by their empirical

interactions, but not by virtue of their common membership in a
single system. The relation of contiguity, designed to bring out the
simple empirical fact of being "given together with" or of "standing
indifferently next to," is in reality the negation of any relation
whatsoever.

The decision to consider only fortuituous and secondary relations leads the psychoanalyst to overlook, on principle, certain essential structures of the patient, such as *the way he fits into the very
heart* of human reality, *the extent to which he is affected by the world,* his
*absolute distance* from concrete reality, etc. These structures, which
give everyday experience its meaning, its sense of direction, and its
range are themselves determinations of a synthetic relation of the
individual with being, which is called *being-in-the-world.* Indeed, it is
impossible to reduce the original connection between human reality and the Whole to a matter of simple contiguity. For if the elements of the system were simply *given together,* none would be able
to break out of its isolation and communicate with the others. And
besides, what does "being *together*" mean?

It means having no connection other than simultaneity. To put it
another way, this *negation* of an internal connection necessarily implies the existence of a synthetic unity of interrelationships. For two
distinct facts to be given together means that they belong to the same
synthetic totality but have no mutual bond other than this common
adherence. The external relationship *presupposes* the relationship of
interiority of which it is a particular case (exteriority is interiority
affirmed then negated). Thus any empirical relationship the psychoanalyst might offer as an example must be grounded in an original
relationship with the Whole, of which it is ultimately only a specific
determination. For instance, the hatred of the father presupposes an
immediate and experienced relationship with the Other. I obviously
don't mean that the child, prior to any contact with his parents,
determines in the abstract his relationships with the Other. I mean
that he can only perceive his father as a person on the basis of a
preontological understanding of human reality as it exists within
himself and outside of himself, though of course this understanding
is awakened and becomes manifest in the course of his empirical
dealings with the people surrounding him.

It would be foolish indeed to imagine that there preexists a "human reality" which subsequently makes contact with something other than itself. Entering a world into which it is inserted at a contingent moment amid particular objects, this human reality effects a *transcendence of its surroundings* and establishes itself, in its very act of emergence, as the experience of a relationship with the Whole. Man is either a pebble or at the origin of all relationships; that is, he is the being through whom relations emerge, or better yet, the source of all relations.

Although some psychoanalysts might be willing to grant this, they would hastily add that it is not their job to study how experience is constituted. Yet that is just where they are mistaken. What we are talking about here is neither a transcendental consciousness, nor a Kantian subject, nor a set of formal principles, nor a synthetic *a priori* judgment. The original relation to the world cannot simply be *given*, nor can it exist as *potentiality*, nor remain suspended motionless somewhere in space. It must be experienced and thereby *brought into existence*. This means that every human reality must create itself and continually re-create itself in its unique relationship to the Whole. Being-in-the-world is an overcoming of pure unique contingency striving toward a synthetic unity of all random occurrences; it is the pro-ject of grasping each and every particular appearance against the background of the entire universe and as a particular and concrete limitation of the Whole. The ambiguity of this relation stems from the fact that it is not a relation of the Whole to itself, but rather the pro-ject of a particular contingent and accidental reality, adrift in the midst of the world of phenomena and which constitutes itself by going beyond itself toward the totality which is bearing down on it. Thus it is, in one and the same act, the bursting forth of a singularity which projects itself upon the infinity of phenomena and loses itself so that something resembling a World may exist—and the reconsolidation of a dispersed In-Itself through a unifying action. It is at once the abdication of original finiteness and the resolve to have this finiteness proclaimed to the world itself as a particular existence standing out against the shadowy background of Totality.

In short, this relation to the world is at once a way of experiencing the pure and insipid contingency of our bodily existence [*être-là*] and a way of going beyond it. For going beyond the body is the only way we can experience it and make it exist. The overcoming of our bodily existence is experienced in this original project, which, as a relationship to being, will realize itself as a form of praxis and articulate itself as a *Weltanschauung*. It is the embodiment of our choice. We get a *taste* of the ambiguous flavor of our arbitrary existence through the very choice which transcends it. This *attitude toward being* is revealed to us as our own pure and ineffable quality, and to others as our indefinable *style*. In short, it is the *a priori* structure of our affectivity. This living and creative sensibility serves as the foundation for all our empirical emotions. Inasmuch as it is this sensibility which establishes our connection with reality as a whole, every one of our emotions and feelings expresses it by particularizing it. For example, feelings of resentment against the father or an inferiority complex—which are relationships with *everyone* in one's world, established through relations with *specific* persons or a single individual—can only link us to the whole of humanity because their original manifestation was based on what the Germans call *Mitsein*. And sexuality, in whatever form we might consider it—even as narcissism—can only surface in a world where the Other already exists. Even masturbation is an attitude toward the Other before being an attitude toward oneself.

Now this existential relation has its pathology. There are disorders of being-in-the-world in the sense that Merleau-Ponty spoke about "disorders of the Cogito" (which is also a concrete and *a priori* relation of consciousness to itself). The ambiguity of being-in-the-world stems from the fact that a contingent existent constitutes itself as a relation to the Whole. The first term of this relation is thus imperiled by the other. And, though a man desires to acquire all his particular characteristics only against the "background of the universe," certain empirical modifications of his environment may lead him to alter his original project, or at least, provoke difficulties and discontinuities within it. Thus, being-in-the-world is an *a priori* since it is the synthetic relation which underlies experience; but it can change and modify its internal structure depending on local and *a posteriori* transformations. This happens particularly when certain contingent, historical circumstances put the very existence of Man in the Universe into question by showing him his own basic fragility or by convincing him of the radical impossibility of his own existence. The death of a parent can be decisive because it reveals, once and for all, the possibility of our no-longer-being-in-the-world as one of the characteristics of being-in-the-world. This revelation of the human condition *as a paradox* can then give rise to far more important modifications than a mere sexual maladjustment. It can influence our *distance from objects,* our intuition of being, our very taste for ourselves. It can loosen our bond with the world, turn it about, increase or diminish our inclination for experience.

In the case at hand, although his premature experience with death must have predisposed the orphan to lament his "adorable childhood with its woods of roses,"[188] although it must have exerted a sterilizing influence on his young sexuality, it is not in the realm of his empirical emotions that we shall seek its principal effect. We shall discover its deepest repercussions in the child's being-in-the-world.

Up to his sixth year, the way he experienced his relation to the Whole was quite simply through the love he bore his mother.* His Mother and the World are but one. This tender giant emerges and vanishes into Nature through a thousand roots and branches.† Universal nature reflects her veins, flushed with water, air, and the fires of the perennial circuit of the sun, onto the soft, naked body of her most perfect creature. The child, almost consubstantial with this Nymph who melts into thin air and dissolves into water, clamps its gums around the swelling maternal flesh and extracts the juices of the earth from this familiar body. The mother feeds on the world and the infant in turn feeds on her. From her breasts "woman flows in sibylline whiteness,"[189] and in this curious liquid Sacrement, the entire universe is present.

When the infant is weaned, he discovers that in the eyes of others he is an *other* and that he must mold himself to fit the "persona" that adults have prepared for him. But the mother's tenderness cushions the blow. His father and grandfather sometimes enjoy giving him a glimpse of his future destiny, but he shows hardly any interest. To a son who already knows that you don't marry your mother and who says to his own, "When I grow up, I'll marry you,"

* Mallarmé's mother actually died when he was five.—Trans.
† Cf. line 7 of *The Afternoon of a Faun* (*L'Après-midi d'un faune*].—Trans.

the father can reply without causing undue apprehension, "When you grow up, you'll do as your father did." In either case, the words serve the function of strengthening existing ties more than of saying something about the future. The child interprets his father's prediction as an immediate promotion. Telling him that *one day* he will replace his father is a way of giving him the opportunity to *at once* identify himself with him. As far as anything else is concerned, he takes refuge *from everyone* in his mother's gaze. He demands that she bestow on him her innermost realities through a process of continuous creation. He exists because she looks upon him; his truth is in her. What is more, she lends him her eyes. The little boy, holding her by the hand, knows that she sees everything and that pebbles, plants, and animals all appear to her in their secret truth. If he looks about with his own little eyes, he doesn't really see things as they are; rather, he sees the presence of the maternal gaze in all things. It gives off a dazzling shimmer upon the surface of being. At every step of the way, he finds again, strewn about in the gardens of this luminous sphere:[190]

> . . . raindrop and diamond, transparent gaze
> Resting on these never-wilting flowers.*[191]
> ("A Funeral Toast")

For him, "the glaze of silver dew upon the willow trees is but the limpid gaze (of the mother) familiar with each leaf."[192] The child and the world of objects around him mutually confirm each other's existence. They are each transitory modes of a single incomprehensible substance, *vision*. Their original connection is not one based on contiguity, or even on knowledge. It is rather a mute affinity which arises from the fact that, as fruits of the same love, they both appear to be illuminated by the same clear light. The truth they share is deep within the mother's tender eyes. The world, together with the child which exists in it, is nothing but a maternal vision. And so, the sweet confusion of the child who first comes into the world is experienced in two opposing fashions and the child con-

---

*. . . pluie et diamant, le regard diaphane
Resté là sur ces fleurs dont nulle ne se fane.
("Toast Funèbre")

tinually shifts back and forth between the two. Sometimes, blind and deaf, embedded in his mother's flesh, he enjoys possessing the world through her; and sometimes, moving a step away from her, he lets himself blend into the universe as an object amid other objects and experiences the delightful sensation of dissolving in her limpid and all-knowing Gaze.

The Gaze is extinguished. The great white body slips lifelessly away. A void opens up in the midst of plenitude. Objects take on an imperceptible distance, the child *withdraws from them*. It's just as if he had been weaned a second time, which arouses in him the sensation of being "an elusive object which is lacking something."[193] The child loses hold of his truth—it is lying at the bottom of the sea with her body. He is left with only a clandestine and uncorroborated existence. Meanwhile he discovers the external world; but he gets no pleasure out of this discovery. Previously, the child lived quite heedlessly amid the familiar furnishings and gardens whose truth was concentrated in a single Gaze. Truth was merely a certain way of existing elsewhere in those all-seeing eyes. The actor knows that the invisible battery of lights surrounding him is really, from the audience's perspective, the parapet of Elsinore Castle. Suddenly, things become more restricted. They acquire truth *in their own right*. But what is this recaptured truth? Another name for the death of the mother.

This is the time of life when the most active of his little playmates start looking out from behind their mothers' skirts and, comforted by the knowledge that their parents are within earshot, dare to begin taking stock of their patrimony. Age-old being, always dimly perceived, finally shows itself, and this prodigious gift fills them with its brutal and strident overabundance. Only when sated do they discover that they are empty. The unfolding of the Whole makes them see that they are that "hollow nothingness"[194] which only the Whole is capable of filling. Just as for Gide's Ménalque[195] "each fountain shows them a thirst," they will come to know their hunger by satisfying it. Here they hurl themselves against being and turn themselves into an insatiable craving for it. The orphan is equally aware of his thirst, of the fact that he *is* thirst. But this thirst has nothing to do with the World. His development came to a halt several days or months before that *necessary* moment when one tears oneself away from one's parents' arms in order to turn outward.

The progressive liberation will not take place: his mother had jealously kept its secret. The very opposite happens: like those children who give up when faced with too arduous a task and attempt to regress to a previous stage, he tries to recapture her former embraces. Without seeing her, he contemplates his mother at the dressing table where she used to sit. An old habit makes him conjure up a beloved presence in the swivel mirror or in the chair. Being is present there, but only implicitly. It is the framework of this futile quest, its backdrop. Thus the self's pro-ject toward the Whole breaks down before reaching its goal. A mere backdrop, the real is only a superfluous presence, and it attracts only peripheral attention. Of course, the child discovers that he is a transcendence, an appeal, a desire; but this desire is directed toward someone dead, toward the past. This new *person* who has just been born embodies a peculiar type of relationship, one of whose terms is constituted by a need and the other by a void. The world stays in the background. Reality remains a pale presence on whose surface there hovers an absence. Sometimes it seems as if a form might emerge from this dark shape, that hidden in the shadows, a wing will start flapping, that the downy whiteness of feathers will begin to flutter. In this cloud, in this shadow quivering on the leaves, the Departed One might perhaps materialize. In short, an object stands out, a real object of the most refined and volatile nature possible; but it is not considered in its own right. It is only a means of seeking the tangible presence of the one who has died;

So fair,
Their ethereal rosy flesh, that it floats in air
Languishing in drowsy slumber.*[196]
*(The Afternoon of a Faun)*

But the miraculous presence soon fades away, disclosing the "certainty that all beings are alike":[197]

Was it a dream I loved?
My doubt, laid down by night gone by,

---

*                       Si clair,
Leur incarnat léger, qu'il voltige dans l'air
Assoupi de sommeils touffus.
*(L'Après-midi d'un faune)*

Takes form in many a subtle branch
Which yet remains the very glade itself,
And proves, alas, that my solitude's triumphal gift
Was but a semblance of the rose.*[198]

*(The Afternoon of a Faun)*

The appearance of the real *is* the staggering disappearance of hope. The absolute presence of Everything *is* the universal absence of someone in particular. The emergence of a specific object is the end result of a disappointment, the ashes and cinders which remain after the flames of a dream have died out. All objects are equally *meaningless* and their universal equivalence arises from the fact that their appearance is grounded in the same negation. They all possess the identical formal quality of *not being* the wished-for object. As there is neither a thirst for being nor any expectation of it, the fullness of the real sinks back into itself; it can offer no *fulfillment.*

Infinite positivity is the obverse of a lack. It is the *Whole,* to be sure, but is there no more to it than that? Whenever Totality is glimpsed, it is always just what it is, infinite and eternal and everywhere. The child interprets this to mean: "It is no more than what it is."[199] Each thing is always all that it can be in the context within which it is considered. The child interprets this to mean: "It cannot be other than what it is." He gives vent to the gloomy tautology: "Nothing is but what it is," in a futile effort to circumscribe the limits of being by nothingness. Of course, outside of being there is nothing, but it is just this Nothing which puts everything into question. Far from lending itself to immediate intuition, being arises out of the wreckage of Non-Being. This indirect act of generation is first of all the destruction of absence, that is, the negation of the negation. His mother never stops dying, and this sacrifice, stretched out in time and endlessly recurring, is what reveals the universe. Yet he can't help leveling an accusation against Being. When the child strains to restore the sweet natural confusion and wrest it from the grip of

---

*         Aimai-je un rêve?
Mon doute, amas de nuit ancienne, s'achève
En maint rameau subtil, qui, demeuré les vrais
Bois mêmes, prouve, hélas! que bien seul je m'offrais
Pour triomphe la faute idéale de roses.

*(L'Après-midi d'un faune)*

Nothingness, he doesn't dream of explaining his failure by the insubstantiality of the phantoms which haunt him. He reproaches the untoward presence of the World for hoarding all possible manifestations of existence, the impenetrable plenitude of the Whole for excluding the dead, the texture of the World for being too tightly knit and for resisting any infiltration. The disgruntled child withdraws, and his futile desire seems to him his one and only truth. He affirms the infinite superiority of what ought to be over what merely is. Frustrated and betrayed at every turn, he asserts his desperate wish to bring the dead back to life; and since the world, silent and unsettling, looms on the horizon of his failure, he will prefer this repeated failure to the triumph of the real. This rift in his innermost self, this hyperactive void is his one and only reason for being.

Thus being shrivels up. Garden, statues, passing figures, all slip into the background. Somber and motionless, the world floats in a dull pool of Nothingness. All these familiar objects, cast in solid being, have a hollow ring; they are riddled by a secret non-being. The one who took leave of the world thereby pronounced an irrevocable sentence upon him. From his sixth year, the child will think of being-in-the-world as exile and his life will henceforth open onto an irremediable experience of failure.

Out of this complex interplay of expectations and disappointments, of affirmative negations and affirmations which negate one another, he will later learn to fashion a perceptual technique. It is what he will call "brushing away the dust deposited by the intrusion of chance on the surface of his native illumination."[200] But what is this illumination if not the way he fits into being? Happy children discover the fullness of being as something immediately available. Only later will negation, absence, and other forms of Nothingness appear in the guise of localized deficiencies, temporary gaps, and fleeting contradictions. In short, Nothingness comes after Being.

But for this orphan the opposite holds true; Being is the realm beyond Nothingness. He contemplates the world in the cold light of Death. For this consciousness, being is not something immediately given. What was immediate was the warmth of the maternal breast. Today there is nothing more immediate than the sensation of "a fleeting object . . . of a quivering disappearance."[201] Now all that remains of his original intuition is the memory of an unattainable intuition. As one might imagine, his character will not be an "intuitive" one; on the contrary, it will lean toward modes of indirect knowledge. As a matter of fact, his relationship to the Whole will be indirect. The child, by going beyond himself toward the "nevermore" as his world of infinite possibility, alienates himself in the death of another. On the deepest emotional level he experiences the absolute impossibility of an *Other's* ever coming back into the midst of Being. The goal toward which he projects himself is that peculiar kind of hypostatization of the "no" called emptiness— that calm and soluble transparence in which a whirl of sounds and colors is revealed and which dissolves under his gaze only to reappear elsewhere—that frozen and empty eternity which, during the course of his life, he can neither approach nor escape and which stretches out through universal duration. This original connection between desire and Nothingness introduces a pathological gap in his "being-in-the-world."

In the past, the shimmering of his mother's gaze had concealed things from him; but now he must try to reproduce this unifying gaze on the surface of being. The child gathers up all his disparate experiences by means of illusory and fleeting syntheses, recollecting the trees in the forest because *she* no longer strolls under their branches, the chairs in the garden because *she* is no longer seated in any of them, the four walls of the room because *she* is missing from the house. Thus, all unity remains potential. He makes absolutely no attempt to unveil Totality but rather reconstitutes the Absent One *for whom* this totality once existed in the immediate present. For him the whole is simply a mirage, the bygone vision of two dead eyes. A gap will henceforth separate him from reality, and Nothing will always be closer to him than any feast of the senses. From this time on, the orphan has at his disposal two negative registers; the light of Truth dissolves the maternal shade, and the corrosive light of Value dissipates the meaningless abundance of Being.

Given time, this distress bordering on resentment might have faded away. There are numerous instances of orphans who were able to impose this "labor of mourning" upon themselves. Still, they needed a certain amount of luck—but luck turns its back on him. By disappearing, his mother unveiled to him the figures of two fathers.[202] He used to see them through her eyes. But now, starkly silhouetted against this rarified atmosphere, stiff and identically funereal, they appear as one and the same functionary perceived at two different stages of life. And here we have the third and final stage: the functionaries' own childhood playing at their feet. This child knows that they are his truth. "You will be an administrator, like your father."

Now, at a glance, he comprehends his molelike destiny. What he once considered natural now seems to him an abstract and bizarre fate. He beholds a replica of his future self standing before him, mimicking his career in advance, showing him its tedious vicissitudes. These little gestures are to be his own. What am I saying? They already are. Family life is a hall of mirrors; child, adult, and old man are reflections that mirror one another. He sees his future in them, that is to say the endless repetitions of family history. He feels that their eyes, which peer right through him, are searching for their own past—in other words, his own inexorable future. What is time for this phoenix who rises from his own ashes and who recognizes himself as the seventh reincarnation of the same family administrator? Present time is exile, his Mother's absence and the futility of Everything. "There is no Present time . . . the past has vanished, the future is slow in arriving; in any event, the two recombine reflexively so as to obscure the gap which separates them."[203] But there is no future either— simply the resurrection of old lives. Faced with life relived so often and so listlessly *by others,* with whatever family memories he can see buried in the depths of the future, the child perceives things from the vantage point of death. From this perspective everything is forever complete; tomorrow is merely a mirage; you touch it, and it was *yesterday.* This Holy Trinity—director, assistant director, future office boy (the Receiver, assistant director, and director) in the Office of Records and Deeds—marks out the three necessary stages of its temporal evolution. What people call progress is only the development of order; thus time is but a dream—or rather a nightmare.

Philosophers have taught us—though not without bitterness— that man is always incomplete, always on trial; in order to decide what he is, you must follow his traces to his last breath, for only death can give life its totality. Death makes a whole life dazzlingly clear at the very moment it extinguishes it. This uncertainty has great advantages; when all is said and done, we ought to congratulate ourselves that we must always await what is to be and go on creating ourselves; to live means to undergo trials, to take risks, to discover ourselves by changing the world. What could be better? I wouldn't change places with God, were I given the chance. The very fact of being in *constant peril* can be a source of keen pleasure. The child might have managed to *live* even in spite of his loss had he only been *unaware of his future*. This still might have been possible even though he inherited his father's profession. But in that case, it would at least have had to contain some element of danger, of risk.

Yet this was not so; the Recorder's Office is part of the skeleton of civil society. It is beyond the reach of war or political upheavals. It escapes History. And it is obvious that neither personal characteristics nor the events of private life will have any bearing on one's future career. What do personal worth, work, or even intrigues matter? If you are not chosen for promotion, you will get it through seniority. There is no risk whatsoever. "Good friends in high places can easily advance his career."* There is no need for talent or for any special calling: "It is not absolutely necessary to have any inclination for a career in order to succeed in it. You should above all be guided by good sense and know how to take advantage of opportunities."† Yes, especially if there is still *something* which has not yet been completely decided. It is not clear whether one will end up as director or assistant director. The imperceptible distance separating his father from his grandfather—that covers the entire range of uncertainty and the stakes of an entire lifetime. Had they at least hated their profession, had they viewed it as the very image of their abject slavery, then his curse might possibly have brought them to life and the child might then have concluded that what was important in life lay outside one's job.

But in this family man and job are identical. These jobs bind them like iron corsets, and when some flesh protrudes, it is quickly

*Letter by grandfather Desmolins [to Mr. Lane, 1862]; Mondor, [*Mallarmé plus intime*], 100.
†[Letter by grandfather Desmolins to Stéphane Mallarmé, 25 January 1862.] In Mondor, [*Mallarmé plus intime*], 91.

poked back in with a finger, like a shirttail which has slipped out of
a fly. Since he will grow up to be a functionary and since the
functionary is already a finished product, this black-clad orphan,
standing between these two gentlemen also clad in black and looking like his brothers, feels that he is now fully formed. The life
standing there before him is a closed, circular, and finite totality. If
he wants to see its outcome, he merely has to look up—it will be
either the assistant director's premature senility or the grandfather's moral pedantry. And inasmuch as the sum total of life is
found only in death, the child, not content to view the outside
world through his mother's death, views the unfolding of his life
from the vantage point of his own death. He himself embodies that
paradoxical moment which both produces and effaces the sum
total of his existence.

The fact remains that one must go on living—that is, to *pass time*.
This time is pure, devoid of content; for no storm ever comes along
to blow away the clouds. Passages of poetry learned by heart run
through his mind, all too familiar essences become real, but their
coming into being adds so little to them that it is unclear whether he
is actually experiencing them or merely contemplating them. The insipid taste of moments which are always empty, always indistinguish-
able from one another, is called *ennui*. The child politely lends an ear
to interminable stories he has heard a hundred times before. He is
no longer sure whether he is remembering or really hearing these
old wearisome phrases. He stifles a yawn and politely feigns interest
in the details. Concealed within this child, already dead at the age of
ten, is a secret decrepitude and the experience of a century.[204]

Someone else might have thought of rebelling. This child, however, deprived himself of the means to do so. In her absence, his
mother embodies the hollow futility of everything; nothing escapes
her damning verdict, which can never be appealed. Moreover, her
verdict produces contradictory results: it reveals the absurdity of
his personal destiny while preventing him from rising up against it.
It would be attaching far too much importance to some particular
circumstance of life to want to change *it* rather than another. This
orphan is caught in a trap. He is nothing but a cult of absence and
his mother has become his unique object of devotion. He will res-
cue this singular figure from oblivion; by the sheer strength of his

despair he will maintain this tender silence against the deceitful chatter of people and things.

But this ambiguous phantom proves to be quite irreplaceable, like those possessed nuns who, with a kiss, are transformed into skeletons. It turns into abstract universality whenever the child tries to behold it. For the singularity of the dead mother, now that her grace and flesh are buried, is *precisely* the impossibility of her existing anywhere in time and space. And since he must bear witness for her, the child forbids himself from having to do with anything other than the hypostatized negation of each particular object, that is to say, the empty form of universality. This is how the mystification operates: with outstretched arms, he throws himself toward something ineffable, toward pure singularity; he embraces only the pure concept of negativity which screens him from the endless swarming of concrete forms, each one of which vainly solicits from him its own special acceptance or refusal. In short, he cannot complain, not even to himself, of the incomparable horror of his predicament. He cannot even conceive it, and yet he cannot help suffering from it most acutely. It is a strange kind of suffering, one which turns into stoic exile whenever he tries to focus on it. It is also a strange kind of latent and muffled revolt which will never take place, since it cannot take on any concrete form. He is dying of tedium and dread, the family past weighs on him with "an overwhelming sensation that it's all over,"[205] but he lacks even the words to name this loathing. No sooner does it appear than it seems to him merely an indictment of the inadequacy of the universe.

Feelings of anger which are hastily suppressed, feelings of indignation which are *borne in silence,* a frozen sterility whose icy crust hides an uneasiness which dares not pronounce its name: this is his inner life. Occasionally, he allows himself a brief, cold outburst of temper: "All these people will pay for what they did to me, for my poems will be bitter pills for them—I will deprive them of Paradise."[206] Sometimes, at the height of his anger, he speaks to himself as if he were *someone else,* a future murderer:

> They will make you evil and one day you will commit a crime. . . . Your head still stands attached to your shoulders and wants to leave you as if, while you carry on with an ever

more menacing air, it already knew its fate. It will bid you adieu when you have paid back those less worthy than I. That is probably why you came into the world.[207]

At once murder and martyrdom,* this killing is in reality a suicide. Later he will confirm this: to kill (oneself or another) is the only possible form of action one can take.[208] But no sooner does this hatred come to life than it is coldly extinguished. The child apologizes:

> They covet hatred and feel only rancor.[209]
> ("The Jinx")

So many false alarms, so many counterfeit heartthrobs: feathers mysteriously ruffle, then vanish. The anger he feels dissolves into an anger he merely thinks about and finally into an anger he rejects. Later, we shall encounter the same mystifying visitations as they relate to the sources of his inspiration. This child is not insensitive; but his sensitivity has become involved in such an abstract adventure that his concrete feelings and, more generally, all the particular modes of his consciousness have the utmost difficulty in expressing themselves.

Whenever his hatred subsides, he is overcome by a coldheartedness and a sense of sterility which increase with each passing day. He becomes, quite literally, a block of ice. In 1853 Madame Desmolins, his grandmother, begins complaining that she can see in him the first signs of adolescent self-centeredness. In 1854 "he no longer has a very nice character; he has gone into his difficult phase."[210] By 1858 she "finds him so heartless and so arid that [she] hardly dares rely on him."[211] His schoolmasters deplore "his vain and insubordinate character, which drives him to constant disobedience, to a point of refusing to admit that he could ever be at fault."[212] In 1860 Madame Desmolins again laments: "I sadly look on as he wears his grandfather out, and since his tastes are nothing like ours, he can find no entertainment here."[213] And

---

*This also is a symbol of the decapitated martyr—see Canticle of Saint John (Cantique de Saint Jean).

"the poor child also has a long way to go to become sociable and to acquire some social graces."[214]

In point of fact, the orphan seems not to have borne his grandparents much affection. It is true that in 1885 he will write that he was "worshipped by a grandmother who raised him from infancy."[215] This, however, was just a manner of speaking. To begin with, Madame Desmolins *didn't worship him.* She certainly loved him in her whining and grumbling way, but with no real understanding. As for him, ashamed for having blamed the worst things on his father's second wife, he will one day seek pardon—he is now twenty-two— with these simple words: "She was under the inquisitorial influence of my grandmother, that's all."[216] The second wife terrorized by the mother of the first—there, in a few strokes, is the totally black family portrait. Though nothing the child had to say about grandfather Desmolins has come down to us, read the letters he sent him in 1862: their stiff courtesy is unable to conceal his deep-seated animosity.[217]

A bit later, on the occasion of his dear grandfather's death, he will send his young wife a letter which does not appear to express any real emotion. But the fact is that he willingly conceals his indifference out of simple politeness or his animosity beneath a sentiment appropriate to the occasion. He is closest to the truth when, a few days after the funeral, he writes to a friend: "The death of my poor grandfather has robbed me of a rich source of reverie";[218] and he comes still closer when, thinking of the two losses he has suffered, he declares:

> But, blazon of mourning scattered on vain walls,
> I scorned the lucid honor of a tear,
> When, unalarmed and deaf even to my sacred verse,
> One of these passers-by, proud, blind and mute,
> Guest of his own vague shroud, was transformed
> Into the virgin hero of posthumous hope.*[219]
>
> ("A Funeral Toast")

* Mais le blason des deuils épars sur de vains murs
  J'ai méprisé l'horreur lucide d'une larme,
  Quand, sourd même à mon vers sacré qui ne l'alarme
  Quelqu'un de ces passants, fier, aveugle et muet,
  Hôte de son linceul vague, se transmuait
  En le vierge héros de l'attente posthume.
  ("Toast Funèbre")

His relations with his widowed grandmother become even colder and more infrequent; by the time the old woman breathes her last, she will have almost completely fallen out with her grandson. Nor will the rest of the family find any favor with this "last member of the race."[220] His stepmother is "a penny-pinching angel." "She has but two awful words glued to her lips: saving money. Since she carries these words about like a cat with a dead mouse, I very rarely speak to her."[221] His aunts have a "sad, emaciated look."[222] As for his classmates, they are "hideous";[223] moreover, except for Espinas, to whom he dedicated one of his first poems,[224] we are not acquainted with a single one of them; nor is there a single one who remained his friend during his adulthood. It is striking that all of his friendships were formed after he left school, and that all of them were based on a common affinity for poetry.

One can get an idea of the feelings aroused in him by the surrounding bourgeois society from the following single incident. On December 6, 1863, he arrives in Tournon. Less than a week later he writes to Albert Collignon: "There is no one here I want to get to know. In this black village to which I have been exiled, I can't help being horrified by the endearing intimacy between the people and pigs. Here the pig is the household god." To pass judgment on an entire community so rapidly in such terms shows that the judgment must have been made in advance. Indeed, we read in his correspondence that the bourgeois are "hideous" and "soulless."[225]

Do the workers, at least, come in for any kinder treatment? Not at all. The boy shows no concern for social and political issues: "I don't like the workers. They are too conceited."[226] Only one conclusion remains: "Isn't the man who created the Venus de Milo greater than the one who saves a nation?"[227] Deep down, the only one he really loves is his sister, Maria, because she has been deprived of the same mother. But she dies in his sixteenth year. As a matter of fact, I don't at all believe that her death, which certainly caused him suffering, precipitated the upheaval in the life of the future poet that people assume it did. The "letters to his sister" published by Mondor[228] are quiet and mannered. The one he sends her on the occasion of her first communion is frankly unpleasant. Something about his sanctimonious verbosity recalls the style of grandmother Desmolins:

Dear little sister,

How could I let such a beautiful day slip by without writing you a few words? Though I have very little time for myself, mustn't I make time for such an occasion? I learned with much delight that you have been awarded a good conduct medal. It proves how well you have prepared yourself for one of the most important events of your life. It brings to mind the day I experienced the same happiness that will be yours today. So that no feeling of sadness might interfere with this occasion, which should be full of joy, I did my best to get permission to leave at seven-thirty in the morning to make sure that I could join you and little mama.*[229] After a hard try I also managed to find a good seat for you. . . .[230]

This too edifying homily has a hollow ring to it. He likes playing big brother. Isn't this the same writer who will later coldly and ironically write passionate letters to Marie Gerhard? Isn't he a member of a generation whose poets pride themselves in writing "moving poetry with perfectly cool heads"?[231]

This loss, however, consummates his isolation. He sees it as the reenactment of a sacred tragedy. It is his mother's death all over again. The Mystery of the Disincarnation, uniting myth and ritual, seems to establish a kind of upside-down Christianity: instead of the Second Coming, it is Absence which becomes the object of hope. "In the beginning" was not the word, but that ignoble abundance of being, Vulgarity. What is worshipped is neither the Creation nor the passing of the Word into the World, but rather a whittling-down of Reality to fit the Word. Amid the vague murmurings[232] of reality, a *single* being has sacrificed herself for all others. On two separate occasions her bodily presence dissolved, until nothing remained of it but that aftertaste, the word, a host filled with an absence, a "magic, closed-up water lily enveloping a void in its hollow whiteness."[233] Through his irrevocable refusal ever to exist anywhere, the penitent bears witness to the purest of Beings, who shimmers as a result of his systematic efforts to dematerialize her.

---

*"Petite maman" is the expression used by young Mallarmé to refer to his stepmother.—TRANS.

And yet this Being is nothing but its own negation; its very perfection—an ontological proof in reverse—implies its non-existence. This Being is self-caused, but only in the sense that it *is* what prevents itself from existing by virtue of its very impossibility. In a word, being exists only to negate itself, in the same way that, for instance, we attribute Being to a Void or to Nothingness by the simple act of naming them. The faint, steady shimmering is the non-Being of Being in the process of becoming the being of non-Being, only to be further transformed into the non-Being of Nothingness. Christianity, the family religion, had for a long time crowned that barbarous and refined Manicheanism in which Gnostic games are grafted onto a human sacrifice, but the second death of the Mother pushed it aside. All told, the child never was a very fervent believer. Christianity offered him a presence *elsewhere,* whereas he was satisfied with an Absence *here on earth.* The young priest of the new Cult does not address himself to God; he saves his prayers for a great Goddess who will be the image of everything a woman can represent for a man, aside from carnal love—a white goddess of chastity who fuses mother and sister into a single absence. Nothing remains in this squalid world to represent Nature and Life, except that Bitch, the Mother-in-Law, who is in rut and wants to be fucked.[234] He hadn't yet read Baudelaire's intimate journals, with its famous cry: "Woman is natural, therefore abominable." In 1867, the young professor wrote: "Woman, who is base and vulgar, dicovers that her chief preoccupation is with the most degrading side of her passive and sick female condition—her *menstruation.*"[235]

Henceforth the child will turn inward. His anger against his fate makes him turn the situation to his own advantage. Painfully and mystically, he once loved what doesn't exist and what never can exist. One stroke of the Reaper's scythe had transformed the most natural and simple childhood love into an unbearable and never-ending feeling of emptiness. He will deny the world, set up this Absence within it, and identify himself with it. *He who was once denied* turns into the Denier. Revolt is ineffectual, inconceivable, impractical; but refusal is possible. Even though his refusal will be expressed with much politeness and ceremoniousness, with a kind of elegant good humor, it will be *all-inclusive.* He is bent on total destruction. And since there is no explosive powerful enough to reduce the world to dust, he will pretend that he does not inhabit it. And where might this poet be? *Nowhere.* Actually he is somewhere: he is right here, completely taken in by his own pretense that he has taken leave of the world. This absence, or systematic rejection of experience, is not any sort of real presence in some far-off realm. It is a false non-presence in the here and now. He doesn't merely formulate this rejection; he experiences it. It consists of a giant step backward, such that all one's surroundings appear as if seen through the wrong end of a telescope, while simultaneously giving oneself the impression of seeing things as they are when no ob-server is present. Obviously this effort transports him to a level of reflection. He will manage to acquire the attitude he has been aim-ing for by becoming conscious of consciousness. He sees the world *through* a sort of windowpane and then again, his reflexive con-sciousness thinks it can *see* the reflected consciousness which is do-ing the seeing. Thus, by taking refuge within reflexive conscious-ness, by refusing to make the best of things, we succeed in saying that it is not we who are seeing the world shimmering out there. This position is exactly what is needed, for the child is thoroughly immersed in his predicament and rejects himself.

The problem is that the child cannot accept himself. He was taken aback to discover, within himself, the oppressive virtues of the bourgeoisie, and he knows that they are permanently im-planted within him. A taste for order, austerity, thrift, home life, disinterestedness, and dignity will henceforth become a permanent character trait. Whenever he tries to flee the asphyxiating family atmosphere and regain access to himself, he only finds the whole family sitting there, with its old memories and old furniture. Some-times he thinks he can feel a premonition of another still-unde-finable self rubbing up against him. No sooner does he look in the mirror and what does he see? Something out of the family album. When he is at his most honest, he cannot imagine why he should escape the universal verdict. In the past, his mother's Gaze had "sanctified"[236] his entire existence. Now that her eyes are shut, what is left? An empirical and profane Self which, at the bottom, is none other than his father's Self.

In short, his mother pried his absolute Truth from him, tore him away from the frightful need to reproduce a new version of his

Father. Having lost his Truth, he will at least avoid contamination by this congenital affliction. He is not, nor will he ever be, one of those proud robbers in Schiller's play, driven by self-torment, who set the law of their hearts against the Course of the World.[237] Before ever putting reality within brackets, he imprisons himself within them. [*Fragments follow. See note 238.*]

And so he adopts a reflexive personality which is none other than the abstract negation of his empirical personality.[238]

But there is more to it than that.

Resentment. The Father.

This family, which is reincarnated in him, weighs down upon him "with an overwhelming sensation that 'it's all over.' "[239] He dies of horror and boredom. "The pain I suffer by living is dreadful."[240] But this spontaneous feeling will elude definition and remain unnamed. An icy sterility, and beneath it a nameless dread of his father and of his family.

. . . Especially after his father remarried. Not that he rushed into it. He waited until 1852, almost five years after the death of his wife. No matter. He steals away. He had left open the possibility of allying himself with the child in his total Manicheanism, which kept the World distinct from the Dead Mother. But now he adopted as his own the implacable judgment which Being pronounces on the absent one. He turns himself into *opacity,* contingency, flesh. He chose absurd plenitude and malice. "I don't enjoy myself,"[241] the child would later say. From Baudelaire he will borrow and bring to a still higher level of abstraction the notion of voluptuousness, of gratification etched onto negativity, like a diamond scratching the pane of glass which separates him from the outside world.[242]

But the father decided on enjoyment. He wallowed in the pigsty of being. For that he will never be pardoned. As the ultimate indignity, he fathers a child with his new wife. This little intruder will not be welcomed kindly. The poet's maternal grandmother does not conceal her disillusionment. Maria, his younger sister, is even more categorical: "This little girl is not my sister; she is only little mama's* daughter, and little mama means nothing to me."[243] The future office boy of the Recorder's Office never utters a word about it, but his grandmother admits that she is obliged "to arouse

*See note, p. 105.

his affection for this newcomer who has yet to win his sympathy."[244] It seems that she never did succeed; not once in the years from 1852 to 1898 did the poet ever mention the existence of his half-sister.*

He expresses himself even more freely in his poetry. To begin with, there is the curious "Reminiscence" which he wrote at the age of twenty-three, when already married, and the first version of which is entitled "*Orphan.*" The orphan is himself—he speaks in the first person. Yet curiously enough, he sees himself orphaned by both father and mother. A young member of a traveling circus asks him:

> "Where are your parents?" "I have none," I tell him.—"Ah! You haven't got a father, but I do. If you only knew what fun a father can be—always laughing. Just the other evening, after my brother's burial, the funny faces he made when the ringmaster slapped and kicked him were funnier than ever. Yes, my dear friend! . . . I'm really amused by Papa. . . . Parents are funny people who make us laugh."[245]

The themes of this poem are rather tangled. The poet is most certainly both narrator and mountebank, for in the second version he calls the latter a "kid who is too unstable to belong to his race." He is consequently at once made into an orphan and endowed with parents. The latter, moreover, surely represents the "vagabonds" or "mountebanks" whom the poet, faithful to a theme fashionable since the time of Baudelaire, considers as his brothers. When, in this connection, Mondor recalls "The Chastized Clown" and "The Jinx," he is likewise correct. Yet when all is said and done the grotesque father, who makes funny faces when slapped and who plays the clown even after his son has died, is quite simply the poet's father as well. A curious correction found in the second version corroborates this reading. Here, there is no mention of a "little brother who died" but rather of one "who refused to eat his soup the other week." Perhaps this was done to avoid triteness or reference to Anatole's death;[246] but mostly not to be too hard on the father because, with time, a sort of reconciliation takes place. The fact remains that the child hated

---

*A final statement on this subject cannot be made prior to the publication of Mallarmé's complete correspondence.[247]

his father so much that he considered it scandalous to be his progeny. Of course, it must be kept in mind that the wife is not the poet's
mother, but rather his stepmother. But the emphasis is given to the
father, who heedlessly sired a child. He bears the true responsibility
for that birth. The fact is that his mother's death left the child's vague
and natural existence exposed and vulnerable.

At this same time the father, by remarrying, proves his lack of
worth and provides the tangible evidence for his own child's *carnal*
nature; by engendering him, his father establishes his child's ties to
the world and to Being. To put it another way, the child's bond to
his father is the negation of his bond to his mother, the negation of
Manichean purity, a carnal sin. In contrast to what ordinarily happens, it is not his mother, purified by death, who embodies for this
child the vague horrors of Nature; it is rather virility, the musky
smell of the male, his hairiness, his penis. And so he distinguishes
two principles within himself. The first is embodied in the death-
like purity which he inherited from his mother; the second, in the
unruly imagination he thinks he inherited from her.[248] It seems
that the prediction in *Igitur* is the very first time the poetic gift
appears *in his mother*. And, through the example of her death, his
mother forbids him from sliding down the banister of the [spiral]
staircase. The carnal principle, on the other hand, comes from the
body. So we encounter the theme again, sometimes in the form of a
Twofold Postulate:

Pulcinella.[249]

Twofold Baudelairean postulate,[250]

sometimes in the form of the sexual act.

> I do not believe two mouths,
> Not my mother's nor her lover's,
> Have ever drunk of the same Chimera,
> I, sylph of those cold ceilings.*[251]

Baudelaire;

Corbière.[252]

---

*Je crois bien que deux bouches n'ont
 Bu, ni son amant ni ma mère,
 Jamais à la même Chimère,
 Moi, sylphe de ces froids plafonds.
(Mallarmé: "Triptyque I"; cf. Baudelaire, Corbière.)

We see by the words "her lover" that the poet rejects the father. He is not even "my" father. He is nothing: "her lover." In short, the father represents birth and the mother death.

It is quite clear that he will develop an *antivirile* attitude.

It is quite clear that later on he will display voyeuristic and oral sexual propensities. He would like to see women making love to one another, to behave as a woman with women, or to be treated as a woman (*Hebe*).[253] This is not an identification with his mother (that would be foolish; he respects her too much; he is at once her terrestrial witness and her memorial; his desire is to exist through and for her—not to be her), but a hatred of the sacrilegious father. To be the female substance. At bottom, this means to deny his being by putting on a role. For it is precisely his father whom he encounters within himself—in the guise of progenitor, of destiny, but also of a particular essence, heredity, etc.

What is to be done? To take it upon himself. The child's spontaneous project, which is a Love of what does not exist and cannot exist, his strict adherence to a rigid law, ultimately implies a more or less conscious negation of all that is. Involved in his search for an elusive mother, the child loses his sense of himself and awakens to find himself drowning in it, soiled by it. He then raises this consequence into a principle. He refuses being.

I would point out that these remarks (about mothers and birth) are typical of the period. The theme of the family is necessarily a basic one in poetry during this period, when the new (nuclear) type of bourgeois family is strengthening its ties. Consciously or unconsciously, it refuses to acknowledge that it is destined to be fragmented by Communism, Fascism, or American Capitalism; and that it can no longer hold out against society, of which it no longer constitutes a vital element. On the contrary, this is the period when Bourget and Le Play[254] emphasize the function of the family as a social unit, etc. By his very nature, the writer is an outcast from his family, as in other periods he would be an outcast of the City (Dante), or an outcast from his class. In short, he bears witness to an integration which can never take place. With him, the family tried and failed to make itself whole. The one who feels the contradictions between the outdated snobbishness of the aristocratic family and the new reality is destined for poetry. When André Gide bluntly declared, "Families, I hate you!"[255] the battle was lost for good. And who are the three most outstanding poets? Poe: he despised his childhood and his mother; Baudelaire: father died, mother remarried; and now this young schoolteacher whose mother died and whose father remarried. This is no accident.

Don't get me wrong; I am not saying that it was sufficient or even necessary to have undergone family misfortunes in order to become a poet in 1880. I am simply saying that the symbol was established through three men who had experienced failure in their family relationships, and that their tragedy has a direct social meaning, for it could not have taken place under other conditions. Such remarriages were precluded in families during the Ancien Régime, when people only remarried for land. But there is more to it than that. During this entire period, poets are *sons*, that is to say, they were determined by a knowledge of what had gone on before them. Such was the curious outcome of a history which abruptly revealed itself in all its splendor and cruelty only to suddenly disappear.[256]

[Every time the child retreats or withdraws, he will leave a sort of space *behind* him, like that left by the trail of a mime who leaps backwards and retreats into the wings. When prolonged, these retreats will intersect beyond the world] at a point he would call the Absolute.

The existence of this Absolute establishes the right to refuse; but he is not concerned with characterizing the absolute any differently, and even if he occasionally does attempt to do so, he can only discover negative characteristics in it: the "coldness of glaciers," the sterility of metal, the whiteness of the lilies, etc. It is "a desert . . . which has become identical with the distance separating it from its observer . . . a place of Nothingness. . . . Purity equals Nullity."*

This position is untenable. It is a sort of Methodical doubt without the Cogito. Moreover, the discredit cast in advance upon every kind of purpose by means of generalized negation dashes any hope of deliverance. There is but one way out: the child will only be able to escape the fate shadowing him from birth if he succeeds in *creating himself anew.* He need only give birth to a work of art for

*Georges Poulet, *Espaces et temps mallarméens* (Lausanne: La Baconnière, Collection "Etre et Penser"), 222–25.

him to be reborn "from no other womb than his own filial one."[257] It has often been said that in him, poetry and birth are indissolubly linked. Nowadays this is expressed by the trite but forceful phrase, "self-made man."*

A psychoanalyst would say he is a Poet because his mother, in dying, totally precluded any identification with his father. This dutiful son is the most redoubtable of parricides: he refuses the gift of life and wants to become his own father in order to make sure that he has pushed his real father off into the Void. If he looks for salvation in words rather than in sounds or in colors, it is because he detects a secret ambiguity in them. What is involved in the act of naming? Destruction or creation? "The first act by which Adam made himself master of the animals was by imposing a name on them, which is to say, by annihilating them in their existence (*qua* existents)."† Ideally, language should serve both purposes. In this way one could, at a single stroke, use words both to annihilate the world and to create it by words.

All at once the absolute, up above in all its icy coldness, gets its first determination: the child turns back on life *in the name of* the Poem to be created, in the name of his Self, such as it should emerge from his work. The absolute is the pure Self in its simple capacity to receive determinations, and as negation of empirical subjectivity. "From the outset," Poulet writes, "Mallarmé's poetry is like a mirage . . . for what is located in this indefinable realm and contemplated from afar is neither an object nor an external world, but rather the very being of the observer; a mirage in which he recognized himself, not by where or how he is, but rather by where he is not and the way he is not."‡ In other words, the child dreams of entering into Poetry as he would into some sort of secret brotherhood whose initiation rites first entail an execution and then a resurrection. "I am dying and I want to be reborn."[258] The poet is a shaman. And from the depths of the future it is his own anticipated rebirth which imposes upon him "the obligation to re-create everything so as to ensure that he is really where he ought to be."[259]

---

*In English in original text.—TRANS.
† Hegel. Quoted by Blanchot, *La Part du Feu*, 325.
‡ G. Poulet, *Espaces et temps mallarméens*, 222–25.

Create everything anew! Yet this ambitious young man is the very same one—"ineffectual," "crepuscular," "sterile"[260]—we encounter in Tournon. Just the same, he has managed to loosen the bonds somewhat which bind him to his destiny. If he could not avoid being a bureaucrat, at least he managed to escape the Recorder's Office. Nonetheless, he complains of being "an old man at the age of twenty-three" and writes: "As for poetry, I'm through."[261] He is still burning to write—but what? Occasionally he lends an ear to an unknown strain. A poem is about to be born. He cannot yet make it out clearly—there it is! He hastily jots it down—it turns out to be something he remembers from Banville or Gautier.

Once again he let himself be taken in by mirages of the Future; this poem, which he thought he could see shining brightly in the future, slowly slips back into the Past of Others. He reads over his poems, becomes discouraged and rejects them. Nothing really belongs to him. These "avalanches of gold falling from old azure skies"[262] really belong to Hugo, just like the "badly closed hands" from "Apparition."[263] The vocabulary and the rhythm of "The Jinx" belong to Gautier, just as the term "jinx" itself, as well as the subject of the poem,[264] the themes of the mane of hair, azure, eyes, whiteness, infinity, nothingness, etc., belong to Baudelaire. And it will turn out that the construction of *The Afternoon of a Faun* derives from Banville,* just as the Parnassian School should get credit for a certain stylistic gaudiness which mars the beauty of *Hérodiade*. We now know the name of his ailment: impotence. Was it due to a pathological disorder? A lack of imagination? Too high standards? He himself has no idea. He wavers, and sometimes will baptize his impotence "the modern Muse";[265] at other times, he preferred to think of it as the baleful consequence of a "youthful priapism." And, in this reflexive soul, totally involved in experiencing his thoughts and in thinking—that is, negating his life—how can we distinguish between what it commands and what it obeys? This soul sometimes complains of being "purely passive, today a woman, tomorrow perhaps an animal."[266] Yet it is undeniable that it *registers* as a fatal consequence of his own nature the effects of his

---

*The text by Mallarmé found in the recent publication of some of his *Letters* has two nymphs, one blonde and the other brunette, engaging in dialogue. This makes it even more likely that the motifs of Mallarmé's poetry were based on recall.[267]

invisible will consuming itself in a process of frantic negation. The truth is that, having cast his prohibition on *everything* in advance, he has *nothing* to say.

What should his poems sing about? The love he fears and disdains and moreover doesn't feel? Physical pleasures, Crime, great popular uprisings, his family life? He attaches no importance to any of these things. His correspondence is most strikingly bereft of anecdotes or of political observations. What about God? He scarcely believes in Him anymore. During this same period the members of the Parnassian School attempt to extricate themselves from this impasse by ransacking old chronicles. But the young professor scorns such crude methods. History, along with nature and the passions of the soul, is but a collection of accidents. As far as inspiration is concerned, it is true that he longs for it with his entire soul—but also that his entire soul rejects it. Who knows from what mud pit it might gush forth? What ancestral voices might speak through its mouth? No! His poetic Idea, "rather than being a product of chance, ought to spring from its own principles."[268] After all this, it is not astonishing that his head is buzzing with reminiscences. Since Art must be its own source, the least impure method of ascending from their squalid world of reality to the realm of poetry is still to let oneself be guided by the work of Others. Moreover, at a time when signs of exhaustion become apparent and when there is nothing on the horizon to herald a new dawn, culture everywhere exhibits a tendency to turn in upon itself. People no longer think about things but about dead thoughts.

"Aprioristic literature," Gide uncharitably called it.[269] I would agree, but only up to a certain point. Or rather up to a certain date. It is true that this attitude has often been compared with Kantian formalism. And it would indeed be amusing to translate our poet's question into Kantian terms: "Does there exist a pure poetic Reason?" Or: "What are the conditions for the possibility of pure Poetry?" If we wanted to go on with this game, we could put ourselves in his place and reply: "Pure poetry would reject any contribution from empirical factors; it should rather arise from its own pure self-representation, just as a purely moral act determines itself by simply representing the moral law. Poetry needs the autonomy of a poetic will. What I call a pure or autonomous will in poetry is one that aspires to be universally and absolutely poetic." It is also true that the poet has the same preoccupations as the moral agent: finding a motive for his act which is at once both sense-impression and an *a priori* structure. In short, it is the law which commands respect. The demands imposed by the Ideal should likewise occasion in the poet's sensibility a mixture of despair and admiration, which in turn gives rise to an attempt to bring the poem to fruition—except that in Kant the moral law exists; and though it is purely formal, it nonetheless embodies a theoretical content which prescribes some actions and excludes others. But for our poet, the Ideal—which he calls Azure or the Absolute—is pure Nothingness, the simple objectification of his Refusal. This perfectly inaccessible "X" probably gives rise to a pure feeling in the poet. This feeling, a reflection of his denial, is the stark consciousness of a void. *A priori*, it discredits my immediate impressions and experiences, and denies them the right to poetic expression. In a word, this reality must be experienced in its twofold aspect. On the one hand, there is Baudelairian dissatisfaction converted into an ethical imperative by *petit bourgeois* puritanism; on the other, it is Impotence itself, as a radical form of contempt for others, for the world, and for oneself. The young civil servant's ruminations once again coincide with the sulky disdainfulness of the period. At about this time Villiers wrote:

With his great disdain, he knew how to live and die.*[270]

And Soulary:

My heart is embalmed in its own regrets.†

Later on, Mallarmé's dissatisfaction would assume the more original shape of a shadowy abyss, of a deep hunger, of a constant and silent appeal to authenticity. Yet to the very end his poetry would remain an *obligation,* even when it no longer recoils from the void.

*Il sut vivre et mourir dans ses larges dédains.
† Mon coeur dans son regret s'est lui-même embaumé.
  This connection was made by Mondor, *Vie de Mallarmé,* 136.
  [Cf. note 61.]

It becomes "the ideal obligation imposed on us by our earthly gardens,"[271] "a new form of obligation" which gives rise to "families of iridescent metals,"[272] "an obligation to re-create everything."[273] The poet's categorical imperative is now his self-imposed obligation to create a pure Self through poetic achievement. We should not, however, be misled into thinking that he would ever be satisfied by such a rigorous and abstract mandate. *He never denied* that inspiration was indispensable—he simply wanted it to be absolute. The ideal solution would have been for love to carry out the task he still pursued in the name of an austere imperative. Or, to keep it in Kantian categories,[274] that goodwill should be transformed into divine will *here on earth*.

But now the English teacher starts displaying a very special talent for introspection. Since his sterility comes from his own intransigence, he can at least be sure that it is "circumstantial." Here, then, is the subject he has been looking for: beneath his reflexive gaze, No has become transformed into Yes. Since his impotence will not allow him to write poetry, he will write poetry about his impotence. "At last I have rid myself of it, and I have devoted my first sonnet to writing about it."[275] He would continue to describe this impotence in "Azure" ("L'Azur"), "The Jinx" ("Le Guignon"), "The Chastized Clown" ("Le Pitre châtié"), "The Bell-Ringer" ("Le Sonneur"), etc. How can he escape it? *Hérodiade*, the poem he has begun, does not seem very different from his preceding ones. Yet he sets himself to work with fiercely single-minded determination: "For the first time in my life *I want* to succeed. Never again will I pick up my pen when I'm feeling overwhelmed."[276]

This solemn warning suggests that a crisis is brewing. He must get out of this impasse. Yet he cannot spend his whole life repeating, in every imaginable tone of voice, that he has nothing to say. If his will is so painfully strained, it is because his inspiration continues to fail him. Nonetheless, the poet has abandoned his need for self-dramatization. This time, he decides to write a tragedy. Vaguely in the style of the Parnassians, a princess appears:

Yes, it is for myself, for myself alone that I blossom!*

---

*Oui, c'est pour moi, pour moi, que je fleuris, déserte!

Once again we are at an impasse. Beneath the tinsel of antiquity
Negation reappears, along with the impotence which originally re-
sulted from it. A voice says:

I love the horror of being a virgin . . .*

Who is speaking? Is it the young princess? Or the personification of
Poetry which "takes the place of love because it has become enam-
ored of itself"?*277 Or the Idea which "springs forth from its own
principle"?278 We go round in circles. Temporarily, the poet sets
aside his work. "I have put *Hérodiade* off for cruel winters. This
solitary labor made me sterile."279 A fitting reversal: his exclusive
theme, sterility, reflects on itself and sterilizes him. In two months
he composes the interlude, *The Afternoon of a Faun*. This sudden
ease need hardly surprise us. Because the unfinished *Hérodiade*
could provide him with a pretext, he lowered his standards a notch.
But, the following winter, he again feels a desperate compulsion to
write, and once more takes up his abandoned manuscript.

He rereads it, and the whole process begins anew. He contemplates himself in *Hérodiade:* "Without realizing it, I gave it my all.
That's the source of my troubles."280 What, exactly, does he see?
*Nothing.* His aprioristic attitude wound up impairing his free play
of judgment. A thought, even when it aspires to universality or
seeks to discover an eternal truth, is a product of the soul, a historical and singular event whose motive must be sought in the contingency of our Human Existence. By denying this Existence, the poet
transforms his mind into "pure aptitude."281 To bring it to life, he
must hastily summon his bodily presence, or else he must supply
this pure Abstraction, be it ever so briefly, with the image of a
concrete reality. "In order to think, I still have to look at myself in
the mirror. If it weren't there in front of the table on which I'm
writing this letter, I would once again turn into Nothingness."282
Meanwhile, safe within the brackets he has put around his life, the
civil servant goes about his duties. And since the judgment negating his reality extends to every one of his activities, it gives him,

*J'aime l'horreur d'être vierge . . .

through indifference and contempt, free rein to do whatever he pleases. What will he do?

He takes on the behavior of all the other civil servants—and the less he feels in touch with himself, the more he resembles *them.* Besides, since his profession calls for polite behavior, since it depends in every respect on the opinion of others, he will offer right-thinking people the placid image of all the bourgeois virtues. His grandparents' air of respectability holds sway over his abandoned soul. Of course this is only a "provisional morality." But every once in a while there is a disturbing detail or a passing incident which is ambiguous and suspect. Will we ever know the whole story of his break with Lefébure, whom he had called "his initiator" and "his brother"?* It seems that he showed up one day in the company of an "illicit companion." The son of the assistant director of the Recorder's Office reacted in typical Desmolins style. Judging it an insult to his wife—who, incidentally, had at first been his mistress, and to whom he would later be openly unfaithful—he abruptly breaks off a friendship of ten years' standing.

So abruptly, in fact, that we are led to wonder whether the radical Nihilism professed by the poet was not a mere pretext for allowing the schoolmaster to garb himself in the trappings of conformity. But not really—or only in brief flashes. He suffers. And his only remaining claim to election are the paper dolls which his pupils have pinned on his cape. Would they heckle him if his conformism itself didn't seem suspect? For the time being he falls to pieces. What is left of his previous self are two Voids mutually canceling each other out. The first repudiates the second in the name of the Truth, reproaching it for being "that Dream which Matter knows it is not";[283] the second repudiates the first in the name of Value and calls matter "that *Naught* which is the Truth."[284] With what little life still stirs within him, Mallarmé sadly envies "the earth's good fortune for not having been decomposed into matter and spirit."[285]

As a crowning misfortune, his very pain appears to be "circumstantial"; by seeking to be totally unique, the young man winds up

---

*Because the event occurred after Mallarmé's conversion in 1871, it becomes that much more important.

resembling all the other intellectuals of his generation. Cazalis, known under the pseudonym of Jean Lahor, discovers moonlight in the eyes of his beloved and wants to "drown himself in it" so as to "flee from his tiresome life."[286] But this does not keep him from declaring one day, when convinced he is on the threshold of a brilliant career: "Dream and poetry are like two wines which pall after awhile, and it wouldn't be a bad thing if I were to indulge in them a bit less."[287] Lefébure describes himself in these terms: "[I am] a sad, wandering soul, a passive spirit adrift among things, an exile in springtime who feels at home during fall."[288] And there is, of course, Villiers: "The quality of our hope no longer allows us the Earth. Earth, you say? It has become an Illusion."[289] They are all dead, of course; and it is wondrous to see them argue over which one is the most thoroughly dead. "Which one is the deader of us two? Surely it is I."[290] Rather than reproach society, these young men prefer to complain about Being. It seems less dangerous to them to abolish the universe than to deal with the established order. Victims of the scientism then in fashion, they abandon Truth to Science and seek a new domain for the Beautiful. All of them are haunted by a nostalgia for the vanished Nobility. Let's make no bones about it: when they heap scorn on the bourgeoisie, it is in the name of the Ancien Régime. And if they go to such great pains to play dead, it is because they simply never managed to be born.

And so the poet sees himself reflected in *Hérodiade*, and his work appears to him "in all its dreadful nakedness."[291] This radiant Phoenix who wrote to be reborn, who finally takes pride in living (something) "no one could be certain of beforehand,"[292] hoped that he might rise from his ashes and give birth to himself. But when he rereads his poetry, he merely discovers that a disguised death wish was nothing more than a wish for resurrection. To bolster his courage he wrote his friend that "every birth is an agony."[293] Of course. But, in this Idumaean night, it is the agony which stands out, and if, in him, it is the child who embodies both birth and death, it is very simply because he was stillborn. For he put the Absolute in his poem and the Absolute is *nothing*. The creator re-created himself as nothingness. Isn't this simply another way of saying that he had annihilated himself? Did he really pretend to say that only suicide could cleanse him of the sin of living? If that were so, things would have to be seen through to the end. Suicide is not just a word but an act. During those nights in 1865 this young civil servant, alone at his desk, with his wife and child sleeping in the next room, seriously contemplated killing himself.

But all at once, through "dream-swollen" windows,[294] he senses that "the present cycle of the last quarter of the century is totally illuminated by a flash of lightning."[295] The English teacher suddenly finds himself swept up in an extraordinary adventure. He will experience, successively, "moments touching on madness and magical moments when everything falls into place."[296] He decides to commit suicide and sends funeral invitations to his friends. He suffers in mind and body until that day when, reflected in his Venetian mirror, he just catches a glimpse of a new person, "Slight in stature":[297]

[The humble concerns of the English teacher][298] turn into ecstasy: "There is that moment of youth when you can see your entire future light up before you—not only your own but mankind's as well."[299] The Mallarmé case, which until now has been dragging through the lower courts, is suddenly brought before the Highest Tribunal. A civil servant who wanted to write but was unable to do so realizes that he is nothing less than Man himself. His private concerns now take on a universal significance. In the person of Mallarmé, Man can have no existence without first creating a work of art. In *Hérodiade*, only when it has succeeded in creating its own creator *ex nihilo* can human creation escape contingency. Before starting work on anything, the craftsman must first create himself, modeling himself on the Ideal form of his creation. The Work of Art, through the agency of Man, and Man, through the agency of the Work of Art, draw themselves out of Nothingness.[300] At the dawn of Atheism and forevermore, Humanity will be haunted by the impossible specter of the Causa Sui and of the God who has just died. Suddenly the sterile poet's torment takes the shape of a universal consciousness torn between an absolute necessity and the radical impossibility of creating. For Mallarmé at last understands: one does not create. "Nature simply exists. Nothing can be added to it."[301]

In the past, Inspiration used to be an act of Grace; Man was nothing more than the Trumpet. God supplied the breath. But now, in a Universe "which is always sufficient unto itself, whether waxing or waning,"[302] and which has been abandoned by a Dead God, there are only random occurrences. Now Man is a grotesque tin horn[303] echoing the discordant noises of Nature. The succession of meaningless events makes windpipes quiver, producing only random sounds. Vainly they try to substitute work for the Grace which no longer exists. *What* can they produce if not random combinations, so scattered and external to one another that they resist the act of synthesis which the poet would impose on them? And what can they work with, if not words which chance has stuck together in their minds according to some archaic affinity whose influence lingers on, long after the original meaning has been forgotten? God shows up again in the guise of Old Regrets, Remorse, or the Absolute, as a radical challenge to the idea of Man. A struggle ensues,

> A terrible struggle with this old and wicked feathery essence, God, who fortunately was vanquished! His bony wings, in a death-agony more vigorous than I would have thought possible, had carried me off into the darkness. Triumphant, I fell.[304]

Mallarmé, or the Unhappy Consciousness. In his person, a confrontation will take place for the sake of all humanity between Singular and Universal, Means and Ends, Idea and Matter, Determinism and Autonomy, Time and Eternity, Is and Ought. From two seemingly incompatible selves, a new, "ambiguous Self"[305] will emerge: the schoolteacher heckled by his pupils becomes the new Prometheus, the hero of an ontological drama; the humiliated functionary, never daunted by the certainty of failure, proposes to replace God; the man of resentment, who bravely and modestly accepts the solemn consecration which centuries of human History have ordained, "the only one in whose name social change and revolution came to pass so he might rise to freely give his life and understanding";[306] the impotent man who lends his eyes and mind to Poetry and to Humanity so they might unite with open eyes at last, and who helps them stake everything in one last throw of the dice; the dreamer, always in a fog and forever absent, who is unafraid to write: "I am a capacity which the spiritual universe possesses for seeing and developing itself out of what I once was."[307] And if you should ask this frail dandy, so like a woman, for his credentials, he will first apologize for his roundabout way of reaching his conclusion: "All this was not discovered through the normal development of my faculties but through the sinful, hurried, satanic and above all *facile* path of the Abolition of my Self, which produced not strength but a sensibility inevitably leading me to my destination. Personally, I am without any merit whatsoever."[308] As for credentials, yours are just as good as mine: "Anybody can be the Chosen One—You or I."[309]

What magnificent pride! Aggrandizing yourself to the point of becoming the incarnation of Man and not to take any credit for it; wishing to measure up to God, or to anyone else; everyone's equal: superior only to those superior men who, in a panic, preferred voluntary mutilation to the systematic destruction of their circumstantial Self, all the while clinging to their accidental virtues. It is clear that there *never* was a question of his reshaping himself according to some Idea of Human Nature, or of humbly embodying the Essence of Man. And those who carry on about Mallarmé's Platonism are either dupes or rascals. Convinced, like Pascal, that we are riven by contradictions, Mallarmé never for a moment believed that a human being could become the object of a concept. We do not think Human Reality, we live it: for it is pure *paradox*, a conflict incapable of synthesis. Man is that being prodded at the point of a sword to ascend to God's throne without ever reaching it. Man is Drama, a Drama lived out by Mallarmé.

There were times, as he sat with his penitent air in a state of contemplative indecision, when he could see, shining in the future, a beautiful golden poem, or else hear a strange new melody wordlessly evoking cascades of light in the sky; and when he finally took the risk of setting pen to paper, he would be aghast to discover that *it* had written "avalanches of gold falling from old azure skies,"[310] *a line from Victor Hugo* which just happened to be passing by and which had chosen to borrow this soul and this particular moment in time to come back to life. A dazzling and mystifying drama, inaccessible hence insoluble, it simply cannot be fathomed in a state of illumination, for it is immediately over—in the very moment it takes to reveal the defeat.[311]

This elusive drama is, moreover, at once the transformation of a tempting future synthesis and a manifestation of the analytic past. It is the fading away of a mirage. Furthermore, it is the necessary failure preceding any attempt at creation; or, if you like, the necessity of rediscovering, after the fact, what already existed—neither more nor less.

> He casts the dice, the act is consummated—12 turns up.
> The time: Midnight. The creator rediscovers himself as
> Matter, like the blocks, like the dice—[312]

> We utter words only

> to plunge them back into their own futility.[313]

The tragedy is that man is taken in every time. This time it will work—the unity will appear, the totality, the organic synthesis; chance will be abolished, the reign of man will be established. But this is not to come. "In an act where chance comes into play, chance always fulfills its own idea by affirming or denying itself."[314] What is man, that "fanatic," if not a total and endlessly self-negating impotence who, in spite of himself, still manages to affirm himself? To go one step further: Man, that "potential lord who cannot come to realization,"[315] flashes forth for an instant in each one of us, only to vanish. It's all a lie! Human beings have neither reality nor unity, neither identity nor autonomy. Thought is merely a dream of thought; whenever it tries to become concrete, it turns out to be merely matter, a scattering of words. In short, only Matter exists, in its absurd and perpetual immediacy. We are no more than its "futile forms"—"very sublime," to be sure, for having invented God and the Soul. "But also very absurd, for in us and through us Matter necessarily aspires toward an Ideal which it knows cannot exist,"[316] a futile attempt "condemned in advance never to take wing."[317] For us, time does not exist: it is the rhythm which marks our endlessly recurring disappointments. Man enters time both in the act of losing himself and for the purpose of losing himself. The instant marks the tempo of the Human Drama, the dazzling and paradoxical revelation that the future already *was* the past. Chance is not to be found within Being. It arises with Man. He causes it to appear by setting his Dream and the structure of his goals against the infinitely infinite chain of causes which go to make up reality. We speak of chance each time the supposed result of a premeditated action discloses itself as the pure and simple product of the intersection of causal chains. Man, who brings chance into the world, vainly turns against it. Every one of his actions arises from inevitabilities it would abolish. The useless acrobatics of a self that is forever turning inward: that is the sum total of human effort. The meaningless cycle of generations: that is the movement of history.

Let us return to our starting point: suicide. For there is no other solution. Yet once again Mallarmé escapes. We thought we could fathom him on the level of human failure, but we see that he has already climbed up to the next storey. He is looking down on his failure and making it an object of meditation. We already saw how his meditation fed on his own feelings of impotence. It is from a reflection on his own impossibilities that he will justify his reasons for living. What, in fact, is he? A mere point of convergence among billions of others, "one of the possible combinations of the Infinite in face of the Absolute,"[318] in a word, the wildest and most impossible of contingencies. But also the Heir, the Son, the last incarnation of his race, the necessary outcome of a causal chain. For his despised father now loomed up once again larger than life; he has become history.

Little by little, History and Heredity had inscribed the destinies of organisms and words. With each succeeding generation, the conflict in each of us became more intense, pitting a purity whose demands were each day becoming more aggressive against a Contingency whose presence was each day becoming more obvious. Yet in spite of this, poets went on blissfully. This was the era of Beauty, "consummate and impassive, unique and immutable."[319] And then "Beauty, its heart pierced by the Chimera since the advent of Christianity, [reawakens] with a smile full of mystery, but a forced mystery which it *feels* is the condition of its being."[320] It was inevitable that, after the death of God, the old Dream of the Absolute should have to contend with its absolute denial in all its unyielding obstinacy. It was inevitable that the combustible mixture producing all these conflicts should explode in one memorable conflagration.

This conflagration was nothing other than Mallarmé himself. This useless product of blind chance and last offspring of his race, a "Self projected into the absolute,"[321] this monster bent on self-destruction, is but a culmination of a long madness. His ancestors, "laden with contingency, lived only on their future."[322] But now the consequences of all this come together in the person of a pitiful soul "cast out of time by his race"[323] who, even as an adolescent, found himself projected "onto the summit of the spiral" and who remained there, transfixed, "unable to budge."[324] In him, the conflict could not help but come to a head. Poetry had to fulfill itself and, in so doing, abolish itself. In other words, it had to become critically self-conscious Poetry. "Above all else, the modern poet is a *critic*. That's what I observe in myself. I created my work exclusively through a process of *elimination,* and whatever truth emerged in the process only did so with the loss of an impression which, after flaring up for a brief instant, burned itself out."[325]

Propelled by his race into the realm of the Absolute, Mallarmé conceived Poetry in its true form, which is pure Negation. But his particular formulation of the concept, as the negation of the negation, was the revelation of Man to him. It is no accident that I employ the Hegelian vocabulary here. Mallarmé, who knew Hegel through Villiers, looks to him if not for a system (contemporary materialism had influenced him too strongly for that), then at least for a terminology. And he is inspired by Hegel when he describes critical Beauty as "having rediscovered its *correlative phases* in the entire Universe through the science of man, which endowed it with the last word . . . as smiling mysteriously . . . with the eternal serenity of a rediscovered Venus de Milo; as having fathomed the Idea behind the Mystery which the Mona Lisa could only sense with foreboding."[326] A Hegelian rhythm can be detected in these three moments of Beauty: a serenity in the immediate present; a passage to the uneasy realm of the meditated; a reconciliation of the in-itself and the for-itself in the Absolute-subject. There is only one

difference, but a fundamental one: the Absolute-subject here is
Mallarmé.

There is no doubt that, under the "scourge of conflicting obliga-
tions,"[327] he felt that he held the fate of Mankind in his hands.
Whether or not Man disappeared from the earth depended on
him. Having turned into genocide, suicide seemed to him a "perfectly absurd" [328] act, but one which, by destroying his consciousness and his dreams, restored to the Infinite the personal act which
alone would have allowed him to eliminate chance. By killing himself, Mallarmé could have made the decision that Humanity was
only capable of fulfilling itself by means of self-inflicted death.
Nonetheless, you might say, he decided to go on living. But I'm not
so sure. Sometimes he claimed to have already killed himself, that
he was "perfectly dead."[329] One can almost hear the voice of Father La Pérouse declaring in *The Counterfeiters:* "Since Wednesday
evening, Monsieur La Pérouse has stopped living." At other times,
he recognized that he had "victoriously eluded"[330] "the Unique
Act." These words show that his decision to stay his own execution
remained reasonably ambiguous in his eyes. Of course, it's an escape. In 1868 he thought that suicide (along with murder) was the
crowning human act, the only *supernatural* act granted us,[331] and
he seems not to have subsequently changed his mind. But it is also a
victory—not over death, but over birth. No longer is life that base
and fortuitous gift which had been bestowed on him by his father.
Mallarmé now bestows it on himself because he pardoned himself.
Every breath the condemned man draws is a victory, a reaffirma-
tion of existence. By not destroying himself, Mallarmé re-creates
himself. But he re-creates himself in the form of an *ambivalent
relationship* toward suicide. For this reason, suicide will continue to
be his most intimate concern, his most immediate and intimate
possibility. In his works he constantly alludes to it and, toward the
end of his life, he will confide to Coolus that it is impossible for him
to cross the railway bridge behind the Saint Lazare train station
without feeling the temptation to throw himself onto the tracks.[332]
By constantly putting off his suicide, he made it the permanent
determining factor of his existence, a kind of fixed and transcendent reference point with which to replace the old Absolute.

Why does he put it off? Why doesn't he decide to get it over with right away? It is because he does not want to die without first having actually written the critical poetry which until now has remained a mere concept. Once he adopts as a poetic theme the lucid desolation of an Art which knows itself to be impossible, the circle will be closed and the poem will have become its own object. Thus Mallarmé will have to make the conscious decision to take upon himself the madness of his ancestors.

> I do not wish to experience Nothingness before first having restored to my ancestors the reason for which they engendered me. I would always be haunted by a lack of accomplishment, and that would be enough to leave a stain on my Absolute.[333]

His program is clear:

> To utter the word so as to reimmerse it in its own futility.[334]

He must first bring about the ultimate human shipwreck, glorious and sepulchral—then lay himself to rest on the tomb of his ancestors. This is how the poet will *fulfill himself*. He has at last found a means to justify his race. "(The family) was right to deny (chance) . . . so that (the heir) might become the absolute . . . and Necessary—quintessence of the Idea. A useful folly."[335]

In this topsy-turvy world, it is the Heir who begets his forebears. This means that the happy outcome of this madness will let him perceive the past in the light of "a retrospective illusion." Everything will have unfolded as if the future Idea, plunging back into the murky Past, had in its very absence marshaled its constituent elements. The disaster of man and his death. At last the infinite comes to rest. In spite of everything, this lamp which snuffs itself out is an adventure of the Universe. This is how, "in a state of desperation," Mallarmé will attempt to forge his work. He will proclaim "these glorious lies in the face of that Nothingness which is the Truth."[336] There were times he even considered giving his future poems the title: "*Glorious Lies* or *Glorified Lies*."[337] Once more the spiral twists around itself. Mallarmé, an impotent poet who gives voice to his impotence, converts his personal failure into the Impossibility of Poetry; and then, in yet another reversal, he will transform the Failure of Poetry into a Poetry of Failure. During God's lifetime no one would have dreamed of putting literature, that divine institution, into question. Like the Monarchy, the Army, the Church, or the Market Place, it had an established position in the hierarchies of Creation. Mallarmé was the first to raise the still-timely question: "Does anything like literature actually exist?"[338] It is indeed true that an absolute lightning bolt had shattered his windowpanes. After him, there is no turning back. From the moment he decided to write so as to plunge the Word into an adventure from which there was no turning back, there has been no writer, however modest, who has not put the Word itself into question.

The Word or Man: it is all one and the same. As Mallarmé put it yet again: "Language, which sets man off from other objects, continues to imitate him in his artificial as well as in his natural essence, in his deliberation as well as in his submission to fate, in the exercise of his will as well as in his blindness."[339] His Ancestors, bloated with contingency, encountered failure just when they thought they had come within reach of victory. With Mallarmé, a new type of man is born, tragic and critically self-reflexive, whose life is in decline. This individual, whose *being-toward-failure* is basically no different from Heidegger's *being-toward-death,* projects himself and reconstitutes himself, transcends and totalizes himself in the dazzling drama of the incarnation and of the fall. By abolishing his Self he at the same time hoists it to a higher level; in short, it is the consciousness of his own impossibility which creates his *existence.* Dead and resurrected, Mallarmé offers us "the key to the precious gems in his last spiritual jewel-box." Let us open it "without any preconceived impressions"; it "will allow its mystery to emanate."[340] We must sacrifice ourselves for what we know to be a lost cause. After learning of Regnault's death, killed during the Siege of Paris,[341] he writes: "I am not really grieved to think that Henri sacrificed himself for a France that no longer exists. His death was purer than that. Is is more for Eternity than for history's sake that his unique tragedy took place."[342] And later on, he will congratulate Odilon Redon on his engravings. He likes "this great, inconsolable and obstinate Wizard who pursues a mystery he knows does not exist yet which he continues to pursue for that very reason, out of the sorrow of his lucid despair; for it *might have been* the Truth."[343]

Is not the exile of the Swan, imprisoned in his ice floe, "useless"?[344] Mallarmé would one day express his distaste for "the impious public dismantling of a work of fiction, which goes hand in hand with the literary machinery designed to display either its principal components or its vacuity."[345] When we look at the first edition of his collected poems, we find that a single word sums them up. It opens the poem "Salutations" and is printed on the dedicatory page. Once again it is the word "Nothing."[346]

The truth of the matter is that an experiment must be conducted because of and not in spite of the fact that its outcome is known in advance, and that Mallarmé, realizing that he had embarked on the wrong path, decided to retrace his steps. What could have been his mistake and how would he manage to take his own madness upon himself? I believe it is Hegel who, in a passage from his *Phenomenology of Mind,* anticipated Mallarmé's conversion in the best commentary on the subject. Describing the dialectical passage from Stoicism to Skepticism, he begins by demonstrating the empty formalism of the former. By replacing "Good" and "Truth" with the words "Beautiful" and "Absolute," the following lines will become perfectly applicable to Mallarmé before his conversion: "To the question what is good and true, Stoicism once more responded by offering abstract and contentless thought; the true and the good are to consist in rationality. But the self-identity of thought is again merely pure form, in which nothing is determinate. Thus, the universal expressions true and good, wisdom and virtue, which represent the culminating achievement of Stoicism, are undoubtedly edifying; but since in fact they are incapable of arriving at any expansion of content, they soon create weariness."[347]

Stoic freedom, like Mallarmé's purity, does not reveal itself in technical refinements that have been devised for the attainment of particular ends. Pure form, detached from the independence of things, can only turn back upon itself. Now such formalism is self-annihilating in that it opposes a pure form of human thought to the determinations of life and experience. If they are not to remain ineffectual, Mallarmé's pure negation, as well as the Stoic's, must necessarily return to the realm of things and manifest themselves there in the form of negative labor. The result will be Skepticism, a symbol of Mallarmé's conversion and the very antithesis of empty Stoicism. "*Skepticism* is the realization of that of which stoicism is only the notion; it is the actual experience of what freedom of thought really is. This freedom is *in itself* the negative. . . . Thought becomes that perfect form of thinking which annihilates the being of the world with its *manifold determinations,* and the negativity of free self-consciousness becomes aware of attaining, in the midst of these manifold forms of life, real negativity."[348]

Mallarmé's first move was to recoil in disgust and reject all forms of life in a blanket condemnation. But upon rereading *Hérodiade* he suddenly realizes that universal negation amounts to an absence of negation. Negation is an action. And every action must be inserted within a time frame and act on a particular content. The negation of *everything* cannot be considered a destructive activity; it is simply the representation of the idea of negation in general.

# III

# Requiem for a Poet:
# Mallarmé (1842–1898)

Quite early in life, Mallarmé feels a rebellion welling up inside him which cannot find an outlet. Son and grandson of civil servants, brought up by a deplorable grandmother, he contests everything—family, society, Nature—even the pale and pitiable child whose reflection he glimpses in the mirror.[349] The effectiveness of his defiance, however, is inversely proportional to its scope. To be sure, he must blow up the world. But how can he do so without soiling his hands? A bomb is just another object—like an Empire armchair, only a little nastier. How many intrigues and compromises are needed just to find the exact spot to plant it! Mallarmé was not and would never become an anarchist. He rejects any form of individual action. So desperate and absolute is his violence (and I say this without irony) that it turns into the impassive idea of violence. No, he will not blow up the world—he will merely place it within brackets. He opts for a terrorism of politeness. Always keeping an imperceptible distance from men, from things and from himself, his uppermost concern will be to express this distance in his poetry.

In his first poems Mallarmé views the poetic act primarily as *re-creation*. He needs to reassure himself that he is really where he ought to be.[350] For him writing is a way of obliterating his detestable background. As Blanchot puts it, the world of prose is self-contained; we shouldn't expect it to provide us with reasons to go beyond it. The reason the poet can isolate a poetic object in the world is that he is governed by the imperatives of Poetry. To put it simply, he is engendered by it. Mallarmé always considered his "vocation" a categorical imperative. What motivates him is neither the urgent character of his impressions nor the richness or the violence of his feelings. It is *a command:* "Your writings will testify to the fact that you keep the Universe at a distance." Indeed, his first poems have no other subject than Poetry itself. It has been pointed out that the Ideal constantly invoked in his (youthful) poems remains an abstraction, simply negation in poetic dress; it will be his excuse: the resentment and hatred which make him flee from Being are covered up by the pretext that his flight from Being is only a way of approaching the ideal.

But this would have entailed a belief in God; it is God who guarantees Poetry. In the preceding generation poets had been minor prophets; God spoke through their lips. But Mallarmé no longer believes in God. Yet when ruined ideologies collapse, they don't collapse all at once; whole sections of the edifice remain intact in people's minds. Even after killing God single-handedly, Mallarmé still sought divine approval. Poetry still had to remain transcendent even though he had eliminated the origin of all transcendence. With the death of God, inspiration could only derive from corrupt sources. On *what* premise could the necessity of poetry be established? Mallarmé could still hear the voice of God, but in it he discerns the faint cries of Nature. So it was that one evening he heard someone whispering in his room; was it the wind . . . or his ancestors?[351] It is of course true that poems cannot draw inspiration in the prose of the world; that a poem must have a prior existence; that before setting it down on paper one can inwardly hear its song. But all this is the result of a mystification, since the new poem striving to be born is in fact an old one seeking rebirth. It turns out that the poems on our lips, which claim to arise from our heart in fact arise from our memory. Inspiration? No, mere recollection. Somewhere in the future, Mallarmé catches a glimpse of a youthful figure of himself, beckoning to him. He approaches it—it was his father. Time seems to be an illusion, the future is nothing but the aberrant form in which the past appears to man. This despair, which Mallarmé at that time called his "impotence"—for he tended to reject any source of inspiration or any poetic theme other than the abstract and formal concept of Poetry—drives him to postulate a full-fledged metaphysical system, a vaguely Spinozist kind of analytical materialism. Nothing exists but matter, the incessantly rippling waves of Being.

> Waxing or waning, space is ever space.[352]

From man's point of view, his own appearance transforms the eternal into the temporal and the infinite into the contingent. Of course, *in itself,* an infinite and eternal series of causes is all that could be; some all-knowing intelligence might be able to comprehend its absolute necessity; but to a finite mode, the world appears to be an endless and absurd succession of chance encounters. If such is the case, then the reasons produced by our reason are just as mad as those coming from the heart. The principles guiding our thoughts as well as the categories of our actions are mirages: Man is an impossible dream. In this respect the Poet's impotence symbolizes Man's impossibility. There is but one tragedy, ever the same, a tragedy resolved "immediately, in the very time it takes to disclose the unfolding of a dazzling defeat."[353] In this tragedy:

> He casts the dice. . . . He who creates discovers he is once again matter, blocks, dice.[354]

Once there *were* dice, now there *are* dice; once there *were* words, now there *are* words. And man? A volatile illusion flitting over matter in movement. Mallarmé, a creature of pure matter, strives to produce an order superior to matter. His impotence is *theological.* For the poet, the death of God imposes the obligation to replace him. At this he fails. For Mallarmé just as for Pascal, Man expresses himself in terms of drama and not in terms of essence. As "Divine possibility never becoming,"[355] he defines himself by his impossibility. "The insanity of the game of writing consists in assuming— solely by virtue of a doubt—some sort of obligation to re-create everything merely out of reminiscences."[356] But "Nature simply exists; nothing can be added to it."[357] During periods in which the way forward is blocked by the sheer bulk of a royal presence or by the complete triumph of a social class, poetic invention appears as pure reminiscence. You have arrived too late—everything has already been said. It would not be long before Ribot would turn this impotence into a theory by conflating our mental images with our memories. We can observe Mallarmé's pessimistic metaphysics: within matter—that shapeless infinity—there seems to be some deep-seated need to turn back on itself in order to know itself. To shed light on its obscure infinity, matter seems to produce those shreds of fire, those tatters of thought, called man. But infinite dispersion takes hold of the Idea and scatters it. Man and contingency arise simultaneously and engender one another. Man is failure, "a stunted wolf in a pack of wolves."[358] His greatness consists in living out his flawed nature until it finally explodes.

Hasn't the time come to explode? In Tournon, in Besançon, in Avignon,[359] Mallarmé very seriously contemplated suicide. At first it seems to follow logically: if indeed man is impossible, then this impossibility must be manifested by pushing it to the point of self-destruction. For once, matter couldn't be the *cause* of our action. Being engenders only Being. If, as the result of his own nonpossibility, the Poet choses Non-being, then his negation is the cause of Nothingness. Through man's very disappearance a human order sets itself up against Being. Before Mallarmé, Flaubert had already tempted Saint Anthony in these words: "(Do away with yourself.) Do something which will make you God's equal! Think of it: He created you and now you shall use your courage and your freedom to destroy his handiwork."[360] Isn't this what he always wanted? The suicide he is contemplating has the makings of a terrorist crime. Hadn't he said that suicide and crime were the only *supernatural* acts one could commit?[361] Certain people seem to confuse their personal drama with that of humanity as a whole: this is what saves him. Mallarmé never doubts for an instant that, should he kill himself, the human race would perish with him. His suicide is thus a form of genocide; by his disappearing, Being would be restored in all its purity.

As contingency arises with Man, so will it disappear with him. "The infinite finally breaks loose from the family it has afflicted—ancient space—without chance. . . . This was to take place in the combinations of the Infinite when it confronts the Absolute. Necessary—extracts the Idea."[362] Slowly, with each succeeding generation, the poetic idea brooded over the contradiction which renders it impossible. The death of God removed the last veil: it was the lot of this last offspring of the race to live out this contradiction in all its purity—and to die of it, thus writing the suitably poetic ending to human history. As sacrifice and genocide, man's affirmation as well as his negation, Mallarmé's suicide will reproduce the movement of the dice. Matter is once again matter.

If the crisis was not then and there resolved by his death, it was because of the "absolute lightning bolt" which came and rattled his windowpanes.[363] From this searing experience of his imagined suicide, Mallarmé suddenly discovers his doctrine. If suicide is a successful solution, it is because it replaces the abstract and futile negation of all Being by an *act* of negation. To put it in Hegelian terms, by mediating on this absolute act, Mallarmé passes from "Stoicism," the purely formal affirmation of thought confronted with existence, to Skepticism, "the realization of that of which Stoicism is only the notion. . . . [In skepticism] thought achieves perfection, annihilating the being of the world with its *manifold determinations;* and the negativity of self-consciousness . . . becomes real negativity."[364]

Mallarmé's first step was to back away from his attitude of universal condemnation and disgust. Driven to the top of his spiral, the heir "didn't dare budge"[365] for fear of falling. But now he realizes that universal negation is tantamount to the absence of negation. Negation is an act; every act must take place in time and apply to a specific content. Suicide is an act because it effectively destroys a human being and because it leaves the world haunted by an absence. If Being is dispersion, man, in losing his being, achieves an incorruptible unity; better yet, his absence has an astringent effect on the being of the Universe; like Aristotelian forms, absence constricts things and imbues them with its secret unity. What the poem must reproduce is the very movement of the suicidal act. Since man cannot create but still retains the capacity to destroy, since he affirms himself in the very act that annihilates him, the poem will thus be a labor of destruction. From the vantage point of death, Poetry will be, as Blanchot so nicely puts it, "that language, all of whose strength consists in not being, and all of whose glory consists in evoking, by its own absence, the absence of everything."[366] Mallarmé can proudly write to Lefébure that Poetry has become *critical.*[367] Putting himself totally at risk, Mallarmé saw his essence as a man and a poet now disclosed in the light of death. He does not give up his *all-encompassing* defiance; he simply renders it effective. Soon he would be able to write that "poems are the only real bombs."[368] He even reaches the point where he sometimes believes that he has in fact killed himself.[369]

[And so out of the poet's suicide, out of his "elocutionary disappearance," the poem will be born. Henceforth "words will do their own thing." In their flights of grandiloquence, the poems of Hugo or Gautier still bore traces of the poet's subjectivity; words seemed to be borne aloft by the breath of their inspirations even though no single word could be definitely traced back to its author; the sentence as a whole betrays the impulse of the poet's gesture. In short, it retained somewhat too pronounced a taste of subjectivity. Creation, however, is not a thought but an act: it creates an object which turns back against it and whatever meaning it conveys can come only from itself. In classical prose and poetry, meaning is prior to the object which conveys it. But whoever wishes to create a "poem without men" must refuse to subordinate words to a preconceived meaning; on the contrary, he must arrange them so that a specific meaning emerges from their juxtaposition. Their "inequalities" give rise to tensions and partial meanings which organize themselves into a total, final meaning.[370] The unity of the sentence is not due to the synthesis of a thought which "draws a line" which strings words along in a linear way. Instead, an iridescent and indefinable meaning arises out of the dispersed words. The poem is first and foremost the negation of the poet; it is a *material* object which suggests a spiritual meaning. By replacing the subject's affirmative power with its own cohesive strength, the sentence achieves *being*, not movement. We must grasp it like a tree or a sky and not like some line which we draw. As a reader, I endure in its presence, which is eternal. And since the power of affirmation, and hence subjectivity, is concentrated in the verb, verbs are eliminated wherever possible or else tucked away at the end of the sentence. Thus, rather than being *affirmed*, meaning will be *discovered*. Still there is duration: words "take light from mutual reflection"—there is a "trail of fire."[371] All these words seem to indicate the presence of a sequence. But Mallarmé also speaks of thunder and lightning,[372] in other words, of an instant. In fact we are the ones who move along from word to word; it is our gaze that lingers over these jewels. The succession is timeless in the sense that there exists a *poetic reversibility.* Mallarmé's sentences and syntax become *nominal;* now that it has been cut loose from its author and reduced to a solitary language game, the poem appears to the reader as an inert act, a random juxtaposition which, for this very reason, forever rules out randomness; someone has randomly cast a number of alphabet blocks and it so happens that they spell out the word "Constantinople." A Mallarmé poem is an act of inertia *qua* inertia. The "I" which still occasionally puts in an appearance surges up from the depths of language; it refers to everyone and no one, but to no possible *author.*

Language is present when someone speaks, otherwise it is dead— words neatly arranged in a dictionary. These poems uttered by no one, which seem like bouquets of flowers or arrangements of jewels selected for their harmonizing colors, are in fact pure silence. If Mallarmé had always dreamed of composing calligrams— something he achieved only imperfectly in *A Throw of the Dice*—it was certainly not out of any desire to enrich poetry with some form of expression, but to make sure that nothing is left to chance and that the word is shorn of the last vestiges of its verbal character. Like the illustrator who made a head of Napoleon out of pictures of nude women, he constructs a "listing ship"[373] or Hamlet's cap *out of words.* Merely a stroke of the pen, the word is first of all sub- sumed in its calligraphic function: it is there to be seen. Once it is so determined, meaning is added as an overdetermination. Though it comes first in the subjective order of the composition, it is last in its objective order. By silencing the poet's voice, by reducing words to things—to natural phenomena—poetic suicide entails the destruc- tion of language as such. It also abolishes the reader's subjectivity. The reader, who normally enjoys adopting the author's subjectiv- ity, now finds himself face to face with a hermetically sealed object which he can see but not penetrate, much like Valéry's Socrates with his pebble.[374] Without an author, there can be no reader— just some bewildered onlooker witnessing the dictionary's solitary games.

Not only words, but things too are consumed in this holocaust. During his period of stoic disdain, Mallarmé had refused to speak

of objects and felt uneasy about the unsettled origins of his inspiration. He was wrong. A poem ought to reveal to us the world and
everything it contains; not to *bestow* these things on us, but to deprive us of them. We shall only realize how strange they are once
they have been taken from us, just as only absence or death are
capable of revealing to us the humble virtues of certain people we
have been close to. "There is no reality left; it has evaporated into
writing"[375] *Meaning* is a signification which achieves *being;* but its
pure presence creates a void, a gulf separating it from the word
which, left to itself, tended to become pure materiality. Meaning is
a second silence deep within silence; it is the negation of the word's
status as a thing. This ever-unspoken meaning, which would disappear if one ever attempted to speak it (one cannot recite a Mallarmé
poem; can one recite a table or a jewel?), is quite simply the *absence*
of certain objects. What is involved here is not the mere absence of
a particular being, but a "resonant disappearance";[376] one in
which every absence opens onto a more all-embracing and more
universal absence until finally, just as language in poetic form returns to the world, the whole world disappears from language.
When present, the object dissolves into multiplicity; absent, its
nothingness has the effect of firming it up, like a bracing tonic.
Therefore it will not be named. Of course, as soon as the word
becomes a thing, its meaning evaporates. But there is more to it
than that. This resonant disappearance should be used to name
*something other* than the object being referred to so that its absence
might first be revealed as a deficiency in the objects named. Thus,
the object of the allusive word is first of all the negation of the
allusion. But its absence acts as a synthetic force inasmuch as it is
wholly absent both from the word and from its first-level object.

Much has been said about Mallarmé's Platonism, since the Platonic
*eidos,* calm, immutable, and absent, also brings about the unity of
diverse sense impressions. But Mallarmé, a thoroughgoing materialist, has no wish to embrace Platonic ideas, still less to offer them to
our contemplation; he is well aware that they do not exist. His work
will present their non-existence as a simple absence: they are absent
from being, the way his dead mother is absent from the world. He is
not interested in discovering the ideal and intelligent structures of
reality, but rather in subjecting any object at all to a procedure which

drains it of its matter and enables it to function as an idea, i.e., a synthetic unity transcending diversity. But once again language turns into silence—this time on a second level. This is because Mallarmé's use of words has the effect of conjuring up, from beyond the horizon of the objects he has referred to, another unnamed object whose meaning is communicated *extra-linguistically*. When Mallarmé writes:

Firebrand of glory, froth of blood, gold, tempest,[377]

what he means to *say* is not "sunset." But the effect on the reader is such that the sunset emerges as the *non-verbal* unity of the multiplicity of colors. "[The highest art] consists in never depriving the subtle poetic objects we observe of the appropriately silent veil through which they seduce us and reveal their secret meaning."[378] A poem is thus a hole pierced in Being. It fixes the boundaries circumscribing absence, which, little by little and allusion by allusion, turns out to be the world itself. It produces, in a particular spot situated inside the world, the total absence of the world. Within each line of verse, words and their meaning are dissolved by chemical procedures. The poet establishes "secret identities in a correspondence which, in the name of a central purity, corrodes objects and wears them away."[379]

Henceforth, it won't matter much if the source of the original inspiration or the line of verse originates in some reminiscence of Baudelaire or Banville. It will serve as material for the poet in just the form memory first gives it. He will then treat it with countless different acids until he has created "this vial of poison, this terrible drop" which shall rob the reader of Paradise.[380] When Mallarmé goes to work assiduously rewriting his old poems instead of writing new ones, it is not because he has once again fallen victim to the demon of impotence; it is because he is quite indifferent to his *real* starting point.

Like St. Bonaventure's world, the poem operates on several levels of meaning, the lower allusively introducing the higher. Since each higher level becomes progressively generalized, people have spoken of Mallarmé's "logicism." This is what contributed to his image as an icy artisan of the Word. In reality, we should point out that, like Hegel, his pan-logicism is but the other side of his pan-tragicism. No poet who achieves his own death in his poetry could be a pure "formalist." Poetry is the theme of *each* of his poems (even of his occasional verse). How could it be otherwise, since this is the age of critical Poetry which takes itself for its own object. But since "critical intuition"—if we dare juxtapose these two terms—shows Poetry its own impossibility, the "aesthetic" theme of the poem blends into the human theme of the *impossibility of being man*. The general subject of the suicide-poem is the suicide of Nature, an allusion to the ultimate, tragic act, man's suicide. In this sense, Mallarmé's presence is quite as tangible in his poems as that of a lyric poet in his, but in quite a different way. His disgust, his exile and his impotence, his despair and his suicide, are still *represented* in his poetry, but only precisely to the extent that his personal adventure is an allusion to the human adventure. Henceforth he feels as little need to despise his family background and his physical incarnation as he does to worry about the empirical origins of his inspiration. To be sure, he is a product of chance and of heredity, and finds himself caught, as Poulet puts it, "between a real material world whose fortuitous combinations take place in him without his consent and a false ideal world whose lies bedevil and paralyse him."[381] But the long line of poets which have gone before him has *appointed* him the prophet whose very mission it is to undo the human contradiction. He is *The Chosen One*. Through the poems it inspires him to write, Poetry achieves self-consciousness and destroys itself. Systematically, he retraces the steps leading from blind matter to modern man. Systematically, he attempts to reconstruct his sensibility, but only to purify it of anything accidental so that it is free to reenact endlessly the sacred drama of failure and death.

Yet this quiet tragedy is only the next to last meaning of the poem; ultimately, everything must be annihilated.] It is no accident that Mallarmé writes the word "Nothing" on the first page of his complete works.* Since the poem is both the suicide of man and of Poetry . . . Being must ultimately reabsorb this death; the moment of Poetry's fulfillment must correspond to the moment of its annihilation. Thus, the truth these poems have come to embody is Nothingness.

*"Nothing, this foam, this virgin verse" ["Rien, cette écume, vierge vers"].

NOTHING . . .

WILL HAVE TAKEN PLACE . . .

BUT THE PLACE (ITSELF).[382]

He is known for the extraordinary negative logic he invented:
how, by means of his pen, a lace bedspread abolishes itself, revealing only the absence of a bed; while the "vase, pure of any liquid"[383] agonizes without ever consenting to exhale anything fore-
telling an invisible rose, or how a grave is burdened only with "the
very absence of weighty wreaths."[384]

This virginal, fair and lively today[385]

offers a perfect example of this inner annulment of the poem.
Today, with its implied future, is pure illusion; the present is reduced to the past; a swan then remembers itself and, without hope,
becomes frozen "in dreams of icy scorn";[386] the semblance of
movement vanishes, leaving only the infinite, undifferentiated surface of the ice. The explosion of colors and shapes reveals to our
senses a tangible symbol reminding us of man's tragedy—That in
turn dissolves into Nothingness. Such is the inner motion of these
unprecedented poems, which are at once silent words and sham
objects. In the final analysis, their very disappearance evokes the
outlines of some "fleeting object whose absence was felt,"[387] and
whose very beauty would offer *a priori* proof that *a lack of being*
constitutes a *way of being*.

The proof is faulty. Mallarmé is lucid enough to realize that no
particular experience could ever contradict the principles in whose
name it was established. If chance appears at the outset, "no throw
of the dice shall ever abolish it." "In an act involving chance, chance
always realizes its own Idea by affirming or negating itself."[388]

In the poem, chance negates itself; poetry, born of chance and
struggling against it, abolishes chance by abolishing itself, since
what it symbolically abolishes is man. In the last analysis, all this is
mere "trickery."[389] Mallarmé's irony arises from the fact that he is
simultaneously aware of the utter futility of his work and of its
absolute necessity, and that furthermore he can discern this pair of
opposites which constantly engender and repel one another but

which can never be synthesized: chance creating necessity, the illusion of man—this part of Nature gone mad—, necessity creating chance, that which limits it and defines it *a contrario,* necessity destroying chance "inch by inch" in his verse, chance in turn destroying necessity since words cannot be "fully employed," and then finally, necessity abolishing chance in the suicide of the Poem and Poetry. In Mallarmé there is an unhappy mystifier; for the benefit of his friends and disciples he created and maintained the illusion of a grandiose work in which the whole world would suddenly be dissolved. He claimed to be preparing himself for it. But he knew perfectly well that it was impossible. It was just that even his own life should seem to be subordinated to this absent object: i.e., the orphic explanation of the Earth[390] (which is merely Poetry itself); and I'm not so sure that he didn't conceive of his death as something which would perpetuate this relationship to orphism as the poet's highest ambition, and of his failure as the tragic impossibility of man. A poet dead at the age of twenty-five, killed by a sense of his own impotence—this wouldn't make any headlines. But a fifty-six-year-old poet who dies just as he has finally acquired a mastery which will allow him to embark on his magnum opus—this is the *very embodiment of man's tragedy.* Mallarmé's death is a memorable mystification.

But it is a mystification *by way of the truth:* For thirty years Mallarmé, the "truthful parody of himself,"[391] enacted to the world the one-character tragedy he had so often dreamt of writing. He was the "potential lord who would never become one, everyman's youthful shadow, hence a votary of myth," imposing on the living "a subtle and faded eclipse through the disquieting and mournful encroachment of his presence."[392] According to the complex rules of this drama, his poems *had* to fail in order to achieve perfection.

These had to do more than merely abolish language and the world, more than even destroying themselves; they also had to be the fruitless outlines of an impossible and unheard-of masterpiece which an untimely death prevented him from undertaking. Everything *falls into place* if one considers these symbolic suicides in the light of an accidental death, and Being in the light of Nothingness. By an unforseen about-face, this dreadful shipwreck imparts an absolute necessity to each poem he created. Their most poignant meaning arises from the fact that, while they fire our enthusiasm, their author attached no importance to them. He gave them a finishing touch when, on the eve of his death, he pretended only to think about his future work, writing to his wife and daughter: "Believe me, it was to have been beautiful."[393] True? Or false? But it is mankind itself, the very man Mallarmé aspires to be: man everywhere dying from the disintegration of atoms or from the cooling-down of the sun and murmuring—at the thought of a society he had wished to construct: "Believe me, it was to be beautiful."

Hero, prophet, wizard, tragedian—it is fitting that this discreet and effeminate man with little interest in women should die at the threshold of our century; he is its herald. More profoundly than Nietzsche, he experienced the death of God. Long before Camus, he felt that suicide was the fundamental issue facing man. Later, others would take up his ceaseless struggle against contingency without ever going beyond his lucidity; for his basic question was: Can we ever find within determinism a way out of it? Can we reverse *praxis* and rediscover our subjectivity by reducing both the universe and ourselves to objectivity? He systematically applied to Art what was still merely a philosophical principle which later would become a political maxim: "Create and by creating, create yourself."[394] Shortly before the large-scale development of techniques, he devised a technique of Poetry. At the very time Taylor conceived of mobilizing men so as to render their work more efficient, he mobilized language so as to assure the optimal yield from Words. What seems to me even more striking was the metaphysical anguish he experienced so fully, yet so modestly. Not a day went by that he wasn't tempted to kill himself, and if he went on living, it was only because of his daughter. But his reprieve lent him a sort of charming and destructive irony. His "native illumination,"[395] consisted above all in the art of finding and of establishing in his day-to-day existence, and even in his way of perception, "an erosive correspondence"[396] with all objects of this world. He was a poet to the core, wholly committed to the critical self-destruction of Poetry; and yet at the same time he remained removed from it. This sylph of cold ceilings[397] contemplates himself: if matter produces thought, then lucid thought about matter might just, perhaps, escape determinism. In this way, even his poetry would be enclosed within brackets.

One day he received some drawings which pleased him; of all of them, he became particularly attached to a picture of a sadly smiling old wizard: "Because," he said, "he knows perfectly well that his art is an imposture. Yet he also seems to be saying, *It might have been the truth.*"[398]

# Notes to the Introduction

1. Sartre's biographical study was seen in print for the first time in 1978 in a special issue of *Obliques*, no. 18–19, ed. Michel Sicard. In the spring of 1986, an enlarged version of the work was published by Gallimard. An incidental footnote in Sartre's handwritten draft indicates that the manuscript was written in 1952. He had apparently written hundreds of pages on Mallarmé which disappeared when his Paris apartment on the rue Bonaparte was bombed by right-wing terrorists. The penultimate section of the book is fragmentary—like many of the Sartre's undertakings, this remained unfinished. Ostensibily, Sartre's ambition had been to fashion an elaborate biographical edifice capable of accommodating Mallarmé's complexity. If completed, it might have become a monster construction comparable in size to the three-volume *The Idiot of the Family.* (See *Obliques*, 169.)

2. *Qu'est-ce que la littérature?* (Paris: Editions Gallimard, Collection "Idées," 1964).

3. Sartre, in an interview with Madeleine Chapsal. Michel Contat and Michel Rybalka, *Les Ecrits de Sartre: Chronologie, bibliographie commentée* (Paris: Editions Gallimard, 1970), 262. See also Simone de Beauvoir, *La Force des choses* (Paris: Editions Gallimard, 1963), 179, note 1.

4. Baudelaire, whose early influence on Mallarmé was crucial, prompted reactions of quite another order: one recalls how the severities visited on the poet by Sartre in his *Baudelaire* (1946) offended those critics who venerated him as a national institution. In *The Poet of Nothingness*, Baudelaire occupies an intermediary position; he is viewed as a moment in a necessary historical development which flowers in the unique spiritual product we call Mallarmé.

5. The editorial titles for these sections were coined by Arlette Elkaïm-Sartre. I have intercalated two subheadings (*A Phantom Marriage; The Dead Hand of the Past*) as added textual guides for the English-speaking reader. I have also thought it appropriate to entitle the appended last section *Requiem for a Poet.*

6. Stéphane Mallarmé, "Thèmes anglais," *Oeuvres complètes* (Paris: Editions Gallimard, Bibliothèque de la Pléiade, 1945), 1129.

7. Jean-Paul Sartre, *L'Idiot de la famille*, preface to vol. 1 (Paris: Editions Gallimard, 1971), 7.

Sartre's "universalizing singularity," a methodologically crucial concept enlisted to avoid the pitfalls of reductionism, is rooted in Hegel's "concrete universal." The Hegelian concept is also renewed by Lukács in his aesthetic category of specificity (*Besonderheit*) (Lukács, *Aesthetik*, 1963). For a thoughtful discussion of this subject, see

William K. Wimsatt, "The Concrete Universal," in *The Verbal Icon* (Lexington: University of Kentucky Press, 1954), 69–83. Incidentially, it was Wimsatt who, well over half a century after Josiah Royce (*The Spirit of Modern Philosophy*, 1882), was instrumental in revising the Hegelian concept in the United States.

8. This last section, wholly independent from the study of Mallarmé by Sartre first published in *Obliques* (1978) [see note 1 above], was drafted in 1952 and published the following year by Raymond Queneau in vol. 3 of *Ecrivains célèbres* (Paris: Mazenot, 1953); later it served as a preface to an edition of Mallarmé's *Poésie* (Paris: Gallimard, 1966) and subsequently was reprinted in *Situations IV*. We are indebted to Arlette Elkaïm-Sartre for this information and for incorporating the section into her edition, on which the present translation is based. She surely was right to remark that, despite some repetitiousness, it offers an added dimension to Sartre's portrayal of Mallarmé. (See Mallarmé: *La lucidité et sa face d'ombre*, 9–10, 147.)

Prior to the text at hand, Sartre's interest in Mallarmé was visible in *The Roads of Freedom* (1945; 1949), where some of the characters identify themselves with him. Like the poet, the introspective Daniel is haunted by suicide, mirrors, and tombs. Another of Sartre's irresolute characters, Philippe, turns to Mallarmé because he cannot decide whether to stay put or move on. Inspired by the notion of pure chance in *A Throw of the Dice*, he flips a coin: "A throw of the dice! *Ding*, never, ding, ding, will a throw, ding, of dice, ding, abol, ding, ding, ish, ding, ding, chance. Ding!" Philippe resolves his indecision, leaves, but does not get far: to his dismay he discovers that he has left his suitcase behind. Ivich, Mathieu's young female friend, is like Hérodiade: she can neither stand to be touched nor tolerate people who praise her.

There are also scattered references to Mallarmé in *Saint Genet*, published the year this manuscript was drafted. Sartre found an affinity between the two writers: "I turn to Mallarmé and Genet with wholehearted sympathy," Sartre said in an interview. "Both of them are consciously committed writers." Contat and Rybalka, *Les Ecrits de Sartre* (Paris: Editions Gallimard, 1970), 262.

9. Friedrich Engels, *Socialism: Utopian and Scientific*, in Karl Marx and Friedrich Engels, *Selected Works in One Volume* (London: Lawrence and Wishart, 1968), 426.

10. A glance at Sartre's life in 1952, the year he composed the work at hand, gives insight into its motifs and provides clues to its radical sociopolitical orientation. During this time of soul-searching and intensive study, which "devoured his days" [Contat and Rybalka, 36], Sartre's political opinions swerved toward the organized Left. In July, he wrote the first part of the doctrinaire article, *The Communists and Peace*, where he dissociated himself from the neutralist Left and truculently affirmed that the Party alone spoke for the working class. He had been angered by the arrest of Communist Party leader Jacques Duclos, accused of using pigeons destined for his oven and found in the trunk of his chauffeured Hotchkiss to transport state secrets to the Soviet Union. Sartre, then vacationing in Italy, returned quickly to Paris. He later wrote that "these sordid, childish tricks turned my stomach. . . . After ten years of rumination, I had come to the breaking point, and only needed that one last straw. In the language of the Church, this was my conversion. . . . Our [his and Merleau-Ponty's] slowly accumulated disgust made us realize in a flash the horrors of Stalinism on one hand and that of our own class on the other." *Situations IV* (Paris: Editions Gallimard, 1964), 248.

Sartre's political concerns that year are reflected in the fierce picture of nineteenth-century bourgeois culture elaborated in *The Atheist Heritage*. Henri Guillemin's book, *The Coup d'Etat of December 2,* which Sartre read that year and whose debt he acknowledged, exerted great influence on his Marxist perception of the class struggle during the previous century. Guillemin's study, which drew freely on Marx's *The Eighteenth Brumaire of Louis Bonaparte,* is sporadically alluded to by Sartre. See *Sartre par lui-même* (Paris: Editions Gallimard, 1977), 90–91.

11. W. B. Yeats, "A Dialogue of Self and Soul," *Collected Poems* (London: Macmillan, 1950).

12. Page 19.

13. Henri Guillemin, *Histoire des Catholiques français au XIX<sup>e</sup> siècle (1815–1905)* (Paris: Editions du Milieu du Monde, 1947), 74.

14. See, e.g., Jean-Paul Sartre, *Critique de la raison dialectique,* vol. 1: *Théorie des ensembles pratiques* (Paris: Editions Gallimard, 1960). "In the Age of Enlightenment, bourgeois prudence invented the hybrid concept of Nature whose apparent unity could refer back to the act of the Creator; yet at the same time it devised mechanistic materialism as one of its instruments. . . . The idea of Nature had exploded: mechanism triumphed."

15. Page 19.

16. Page 21.

17. Page 21.

18. Page 22.

19. Page 22.

20. Page 23.

21. Page 24.

22. Page 25.

23. Charles Baudelaire, "A celle qui est trop gaie," *Correspondances* (Paris: Editions Gallimard, Bibliothèque de la Pléiade, 1945). For an elaborate discussion of the sequence and evolution of Baudelaire's attitudes toward nature, see F. W. Leaky, *Baudelaire and Nature* (Manchester: Manchester University Press, 1969), 108–9.

24. Page 34.

25. Quoted in Henri Guillemin, *Le Coup de 2 décembre,* 4th ed. (Paris: Editions Gallimard, 1951), 110.

26. Max Weber's well-known expression.

27. Page 56.

28. Page 58.

29. Page 47.

30. Page 47.

31. Page 57.

32. Page 63.

33. Page 64.

34. Page 87.

35. Page 45.

36. Page 46.

37. Page 48.

38. Page 83.

39. Page 25.

40. Page 26.

41. Page 41.

42. Karl Marx and Friedrich Engels, *On Religion,* with an introduction by Reinhold Niebuhr (New York: Schocken Books, 1964), 70.

43. W. B. Yeats, "Byzantium."

44. Page 88.

45. For a solid discussion of the subject-object problematic, see Richard Kilminster, "From Lukács to Hegel and Back," *Praxis and Method* (London: Routledge and Kegan Paul, 1979), 53–76.

46. Vladimir Nabokov, *Speak, Memory* (New York: G. P. Putnam's Sons, 1966), 19.

47. By subsuming the ontological under the social realm, Sartre places himself in diametrical opposition to Freud.

48. Sartre, *Critique de la raison dialectique*, 71.

49. Pages 79–80.

50. Page 80.

51. For Sartre's monumental contribution to group analysis, see *A Critique of Dialectical Reason,* a work whose richness has scarcely been tapped by American sociologists.

52. Page 80.

53. The term "totalization" here refers to the entire sociocultural spectrum defining the range of an individual's or a group's possibilities at a given historical moment.

54. *Critique de la raison dialectique,* 68. "The given, which we transcend at any given moment by living it, cannot simply be reduced to the material conditions of our existence. Included in it must be . . . our own childhood. The latter, which consists at once in a vague comprehension of our class, of our social conditioning by way of the family group, and a blind going beyond in an awkward effort to tear ourselves free from all this, finally ends up inscribed in us in the form of *character.* . . . At this level are found the traces left behind by our first acts of rebellion, our desperate attempts to go beyond an asphyxiating reality, and the resulting deviations and distortions."

55. Page 92.

56. Page 92.

57. Page 93.

The influence of Merleau-Ponty's *Phénoménologie de la perception* (1945) is apparent in Sartre's analysis of visual perception. Jacques Lacan perpetuated this lineage by the priority he assigned to visual perception in the early formative process of an individual. See *Le Stade du miroir* (1949) [*The Mirror Stage*]. His 1964 lectures on the Gaze, notably in his analysis of anamorphosis, privileged the Gaze as the elusive *object a,* familiar to "Lacanians."

58. Page 94.

59. This expression by W. B. Yeats reflects Mallarmé's influence on the Irish poet.

60. Page 95.

61. Page 92.

62. Contat and Rybalka, 429.

63. Pages 68–69.

64. Page 129.

65. Quoted (slightly paraphrased) in Cyril Connolly, *The Unquiet Grave* (New York: Viking Press, 1960), 58.

66. Rimbaud's letter of artistic intent to Paul Demeny.

67. W. B. Yeats, who created a filiation between Mallarmé and Anglo-Irish culture by embracing and spreading the doctrines of the French poet on the other side of the Channel.

68. T. S. Eliot, *The Waste Land*. Eliot was also marked by Mallarmé's authority.

69. W. B. Yeats, *Autobiographies* (London: Macmillan, 1926), 135.

70. Page 128. Sartre quotes Mallarmé.

71. Page 140.

72. Mallarmé, *Oeuvres complètes*, 857. First appeared as preface to René Ghil, *Traité du Verbe* (Paris: Giroud, 1886).

73. Page 128.

74. Mallarmé, "Sur l'Idéal à vingt ans," *Oeuvres complètes*, 883.

75. Mallarmé, *Variations sur un sujet, Oeuvres complètes*, 366.

76. Page 140.

77. Beckett, in his essay on the painter Bram Van Velde.

78. Mallarmé, "Le Nénuphar blanc," *Oeuvres complètes*, 285.

79. Page 140.

80. Mallarmé, "Mes bouquins refermés sur le nom de Paphos," *Oeuvres complètes*, 76.

81. Page 129.

82. Mallarmé, "Villiers de l'Isle-Adam," *Oeuvres complètes*, 482–510.

83. Hugo von Hoffmansthal, "Letter of Lord Chandos," *Selected Prose*, trans. Mary Hottinger and Tania and James Stern, with an introduction by Hermann Broch (New York: Pantheon, 1952), 141.

84. Page 128.

85. Contat and Rybalka, 262.

86. Cf. page 138, note 368.

87. Page 121.

88. Page 140.

89. Mallarmé, "Autobiographie," *Oeuvres complètes*, 663. On this subject, see Paula Gilbert, *The Aesthetics of Stéphane Mallarmé in Relation to His Public* (London: Associated University Press, 1976), 210 et seq.

90. Page 138.

91. "Théodore de Banville," *Oeuvres complètes*, 521.

92. Ludwig Wittgenstein, "Briefe an Ludwig von Ficker," *Ludwig Wittgenstein*, with an introduction by George Heinrik von Wright (Salzburg: Otto Muller, 1969), 35. "At one time, I meant to include in the preface [to the *Tractatus*] a sentence which is not there now, but which I will write here for your benefit only, since it could perhaps offer a key to the work for you."

93. Mallarmé, "Sur l'Evolution littéraire," *Oeuvres complètes*, 872.

94. W. B. Yeats, "A Dialogue of Self and Soul."

95. Contat and Rybalka, 262.

# Notes

## I. THE ATHEIST HERITAGE

1. These editorial headings have been added to mark out the major sections of Sartre's text.

2. From a comment by Marx. Quoted by Henri Guillemin in *Le Coup du 2 Décembre* (Paris: Gallimard, 1951).

3. François Mauriac, *Trois grands hommes devant Dieu: Molière, Rousseau, Flaubert* (Paris: Editions du Capitole, 1930).

4. The year 1793 saw the execution of Louis XVI (January 21) and the inauguration of the Reign of Terror (September 5), which brought "the high hopes of the revolutionaries" and their wish for "finality" to an end.—TRANS.

5. Henri Guillemin, *Flaubert devant la vie et devant Dieu* (Paris: Plon, 1939).

6. Guillemin, *Le Coup.*

7. Ibid.

8. Letter to Louise Colet, 26 May 1853.

9. Leconte de Lisle (1818–94), acknowledged leader of the Parnassians, is a conspicuous target of Sartre's slings, which are directed principally at his "poetic realism" and his "impersonal" aesthetics. Cf. page 25: "If poets had continued to rely on obscure powers, this unfortunate man [Leconte de Lisle] would not have long succeeded in concealing his total insignificance."—TRANS.

10. "L'Anathème" ["Anathema"], *Poèmes barbares.* (Paris: Editions Alphonse Lemerre, 1947).

11. "Aux Modernes" ["To the Moderns"], *Poèmes barbares.*

12. "A un poète mort" ["To a Dead Poet"], *Poèmes traqiques, Oeuvres de Leconte de Lisle* (Paris: Les Belles Lettres, 1977), vol. III, 93.

13. In his ensuing commentary on the interrelationship between two successive generations of nineteenth-century poets ("Romantic" and "Post-Romantic"), Sartre follows, *mutatis mutandis,* Albert Thibaudet's periodization of literary history according to generations: 1789, 1820 [included here are Sartre's "Titans of 1830," page 27], 1850, 1885.

According to conventional literary taxonomy, the "Romantic" period is represented by four poets: Lamartine, Vigny, Hugo, and Musset.

Baudelaire, whose *Flowers of Evil* appeared in 1857, stands at the crossroads between two generations of poets, and is generally considered the precursor of the post-Romantic Symbolists evoked by Sartre in this work; Villiers de l'Isle-Adam,

Verlaine, Lautréamont, and of course Mallarmé. Curiously, Sartre makes no mention of Rimbaud, who belongs to this period. Could it be that Rimbaud's elusive poetic sensibility escapes his definitions?—TRANS.

14. In "Daphné," *Oeuvres complètes de Vigny* (Paris: Gallimard, Bibliothèque de la Pléiade, 1948), vol. II.

15. Cf. "Le Guignon" ["The Jinx"], *Poésies*, in Mallarmé, *Oeuvres complètes* (Paris: Gallimard, Bibliothèque de la Pléiade, 1945) 29:

If, by his good graces, someone blows his grotesque tin horn . . . .

[Grâce à lui, si l'un souffle à son buccin bizarre . . .]

16. The reference is to Baudelaire's translation of Poe.

17. In the third volume of *The Idiot of the Family*, Sartre offers a biographical sketch of Leconte de Lisle that is more indulgent toward the poet's literary intentions. Cf. *Bibliothèque de philosophie* (Paris: Gallimard, 1972), 345 et seq.

[The range of Leconte de Lisle's influence was indeed extensive. Catulle Mendès, Sully Prudhomme, François Coppée, J. -M. de Heredia, Verlaine, Villiers de l'Isle-Adam, and later, Anatole France, Paul Bourget, and Maurice Barrès were among his disciples.—TRANS.]

18. Verlaine, "Epilogue III," *Poèmes saturniens*.

19. Ibid.

20. In a journal entry of 26 January 1837, Vigny writes that this expression, which appeared in the press several days prior to the above date, was inspired by a passage from his work *Servitude et grandeur militaires*.

21. Mallarmé, "Le Guignon" (first version), *Oeuvres complètes*, 1410–11.

22. Mallarmé, "Le Guignon" (first version).

23. Verlaine, "Les Sages d'autrefois . . ." ["Wise Men of Old"], *Poèmes saturniens*.

24. See his preface to *Poèmes Antiques*, where the poet argues for an "impersonal" art purged of Romantic exhibitionism.—TRANS.

25. René Le Senne, who taught at the Sorbonne from 1929 to 1931, championed a Christian idealism which visibly strained Sartre's patience. See J. Pirlot, *Destinée et valeur: La Philosophie de René Le Senne* (Paris: Vrin, 1954).—TRANS.

26. Simone Weil (1909–43), whose reputation was built posthumously, endeavored to reconcile Christian mysticism and militant syndicalism. See, e.g., *La Pesanteur et la Grâce* (Paris: Union Générale des Editions, 1963).—TRANS.

27. The pun, of course, is on *Left-Wing Communism—An Infantile Disorder* (1921), where for the first time Lenin addresses himself to problems of Marxist strategy in more advanced environments than that of post-czarist Russia.—TRANS.

28. The reference is to the 1848 Revolution and to the proclamation of the Second Republic. The expression comes from Falloux and is quoted by Guillemin in *Le Coup*.

29. Guillemin, *Le Coup*.

30. The reference is to Schiller's drama, *Die Räuber* (1782). [Translated into French in 1785 and adapted for the Parisian stage three years later, it exercised a decisive influence on French romantic melodrama.—TRANS.]

31. Verlaine, *Poèmes saturniens*, Prologue.

32. Napoleon's coup d'état of 2 December 1851, forced Hugo into exile on the

Isle of Jersey. Banished in 1855 by order of the English government, he took refuge on the neighboring Isle of Guernsey until the fall of the Empire.—TRANS.

33. Verlaine, *Poèmes saturniens,* Prologue.

34. The allusion is to a remark by Jean Cocteau in *Les Mariés de la tour Eiffel:* "Since such mysteries are beyond us, let us make believe we originated them."

35. "The poet's attitude toward his times causes him to disown society and to reject the corrupted means of expression at his disposal. He disparages whatever advice he receives as inappropriate to his private pursuits." Mallarmé, "Sur l'évolution littéraire" ["On Literary Evolution"], *Oeuvres complètes,* 870.

36. In his formal answering speech upon election to the Académie Française.

37. Date of Louis Napoleon's *coup d'état.*

38. Cf. Mallarmé, "La Musique et les lettres" ["Music and Letters"], *Oeuvres complètes,* 648.

39. "Woman is *natural,* hence abominable. She is also permanently vulgar, hence the very opposite of a dandy." ("Mon coeur mis à nu" ["My Heart Laid Bare"], *Oeuvres complètes* (Paris: Gallimard, Bibliothèque de la Pléiade, 1961), 1272; cf. Mallarmé's letter to Lefébure, 17 May 1867, quoted by Henri Mondor in *Eugène Lefébure* (Paris: Gallimard, 1951), 347–54.

40. Cf. page 27, "The Titans of 1830."—TRANS.

41. "Thus the first-comers encounter a masterpiece. O golden clasps of age-old missals! O unprofaned papyrus rolls!" Mallarmé, "L'Art pour tous" ["Art for Everyone"], *Oeuvres complètes,* 257.

42. Opening sentence of Descartes's *Discourse on Method.*

43. Cf. page 34, note 38.

44. Guillemin, *Le Coup.*

45. Letter to Mallarmé, 27 May 1867. Mondor, *Eugène Lefébure,* 247.

46. It was the Catholic writer Denis de Rougemont who, in his influential *L'Amour et l'Occident* [*Love in the Western World*], drew a connection between courtly love and the Albigensian heresy, which was subsequently impugned by medieval scholarship. Sartre published a semifavorable review of Rougemont's book in 1939, reprinted in *Situations I.*—TRANS.

47. The *Précieux* movement, with its defiant artifice, excessive refinement, and cultural isolationism, first appeared in France toward the 1650s. Its adherents gathered at Madame de Rambouillet's salon and were caricatured by Molière in *Les Précieuses ridicules* (1659).—TRANS.

48. "Above humanity's crazed herd": cf. Mallarmé, "Le Guignon," *Poésies, Oeuvres complètes,* 28.

49. These took place on Saturdays in Paris, Boulevard St. Michel.—TRANS.

50. "Poetry is an act of devotion. This solitary endeavor, undertaken amid spiritual crises, coincides with yet another birth." Mallarmé, "Quant au livre" ["About Books"], *Oeuvres complètes,* 372.

51. *Les Chants de Maldoror,* Chant premier (pub. 1868).

52. The élite French military academy created by Napoleon in 1803.—TRANS.

53. *Confession d'un enfant du siècle.*

54. *Human, All Too Human,* Part I, Aphorism 137.

55. Cf. page 33, note 35.

56. Mallarmé, in a letter of August 1864, to Henri Cazalis and to Emmanuel des Essarts. Henri Mondor, *Vie de Mallarmé* (Paris: Gallimard, 1941), 131. Sartre's quota-

tions from Mallarmé's correspondence are culled from this biography and other studies by Mondor published before 1952, such as *Mallarmé plus intime* (Paris: Gallimard, 1944) and *Eugène Lefébure*. These letters can also be found in Mallarmé's *Correspondance*, published in 11 volumes between 1959 and 1985 by Gallimard.

57. Letter to Cazalis, 3 March 1871. Mondor, *Vie*.

58. Cf. Villiers de l'Isle-Adam, in *Axël:* "Choosing to live is but a form of self-degradation: Leave it to our servants!" Mallarmé, "Villiers de l'Isle-Adam," *Oeuvres complètes*, 505.

59. The reference is to Villiers de l'Isle-Adam.

60. Letter from Villiers de l'Isle-Adam to Mallarmé, 27 September 1867. Mondor, *Vie*, 247.

61. Joséphin Soulary, "Facilis," *Les Figulines* (1862) (Paris: Alphonse Lemerre).

62. Letter of Lefébure to Mallarmé, 16 February 1865. Mondor, *Eugène Lefébure*, 187.

63. Villiers de l'Isle-Adam, *Axël*. Cf. Mallarmé, "Villiers de l'Isle-Adam," *Oeuvres complètes*, 505.

64. Verlaine, "L'Angoisse" ["Anguish"], *Poèmes saturniens*.

65. Letter from Mallarmé to Cazalis, 3 June 1863. Mondor, *Vie*, 92.

66. *Les Amours jaunes* (pub. 1873).

67. Leconte de Lisle, "Le Secret de la vie" ["The Secret of Life"], *Poèmes tragiques*.

68. Tristan Corbière, *Les Amours jaunes*.

69. Leconte de Lisle, for instance, who had translated Lucretius, insisted on the "scientific" nature of his poetry.—TRANS.

70. From a letter to Mallarmé. Mondor, *Eugène Lefébure*.

71. Viewed by Sartre as a retrograde philosophy superseded by dialectical materialism.—TRANS.

72. Cf. Mallarmé, "Quant au livre," *Oeuvres complètes*, 371.

73. Letter to Stoffels, 28 April 1850. Guillemin, *Le Coup*.

74. Leconte de Lisle, "Paysage polaire" ["Polar Landscape"], *Poèmes barbares*.

75. Leconte de Lisle, "Solvet seclum," *Poèmes barbares*.

76. Leconte de Lisle, "Le Dernier Dieu" ["The Last God"], *Poèmes tragiques*.

77. Leconte de Lisle, "Villanelle," *Poèmes tragiques*.

78. "There is no denying that human life is a sad and petty affair, an ugly and complicated business. Clever persons are well aware that the only purpose of art is to relieve life of its burdens and bitterness." Letter from Flaubert to Mademoiselle Bosquet, 1863.

79. Letter from Flaubert to Alfred le Poittevin, 13 May 1845.

80. Letter from Flaubert to Louise Colet, 4 September 1852.

81. "It is sheer rapture to behold Truth through Beauty. It seems to me that the *ideal state* brought about by such joy is a form of holiness, loftier, perhaps, than another because of its higher degree of selflessness." Letter from Flaubert to Mademoiselle Leroyer de Chantepie, 30 March 1857.

82. Baudelaire, "Mon coeur mis à nu," *Oeuvres complètes*, 1298.

83. Ibid., 1277.

84. "L'Angoisse," *Poèmes saturniens*.

85. Verlaine, "A Don Quichotte" ["To Don Quixote"], *Premiers vers* (Paris: Gallimard, Bibliothèque de la Pléiade, 1938), 10.

86. The paradox is stated by Garine in *Les Conquérants* [*The Conquerors*].

87. One would be hard put to find a more unqualified example of Sartre's adher-

ence to Marxist eschatology in the early Fifties. The heatedly antibourgeois passages that follow are in line with militant Marxist tradition.—TRANS.

88. René Le Chapelier (1754)–94), who drafted the Tennis Court Oath with Barnave, was executed during the Reign of Terror. The law bearing his name was enacted in 1791 and was invoked as late as 1884 to combat labor unions.—TRANS.

89. "Aux modernes," *Poèmes barbares*.

90. "One thing makes me proud—very proud. If God grants me children, they will not have merchants' blood in their veins." From a letter to Cazalis, 1862. Mondor, *Vie*.

91. Cf. "Sonnet," *Poèmes d'enfance et de jeunesse* [*Poems of Childhood and Youth*], *Oeuvres complètes*, 22.

92. "I consider anyone whose thinking is vulgar bourgeois." Cf. "Etude sur Gustave Flaubert" ["A Study of Gustave Flaubert"] by Guy de Maupassant (1884), *Chroniques*, vol. III, Collection 10/18, (pub. 1980).

93. The charitable Madame Boucicaut was the wife of the philanthropic founder of the Parisian department store Au Bon Marché.—TRANS.

94. In "Fusées" ["Fireworks"]; in "Mon coeur mis à nu."

95. Letter to George Sand, 1875.

96. In "Mon coeur mis à nu."

97. If we take a letter written in 1865 at face value, this is not exactly what Lefébure thought of *Elen*, a work by Villiers de l'Isle-Adam: "I conceived of a poem along the lines of Villiers's, except that rather than considering man as too pure for woman, I considered him as too superior; furthermore, I would have condemned him to a life devoid of all hope." Mondor, *Eugène Lefébure*.

98. Letter to Mallarmé, 5 November 1868. Mondor, *Eugène Lefébure*, 290.

99. Such as Leconte de Lisle had done. Cf. pages 47–48.

100. Letter to Louise Colet, 22 September 1853.

101. The family name of Napoléon III.

102. Letter to Louise Colet, 2 March 1854.

103. Letter to Princess Mathilde, June 1867. In *The Idiot of the Family*, Sartre offers an interpretation of Flaubert's semi-imaginary relation to Princess Mathilde that is less discrediting to Flaubert. Cf. *Bibliothèque de philosophie*, vol. III, 530 et seq.

104. Letter to George Sand, 18 October 1871.

105. Letter to George Sand, 6 September 1871.

106. Gustave Courbet (1819–77), the realist painter who was converted to Proudhon's social ideas in 1852, was a conspicuous member of the French Commune.—TRANS.

107. Letter to J. -M. de Heredia, 22 June 1871. Mondor, *Vie*, 320.

108. Maurice Barrès (1862–1923), with his trilogy *Le Culte du Moi* [*The Cult of the Self*], was a zealous advocate of conservative individualism, nationalism, and anti-Semitism. His influence in forging pre–World War II fascist doctrine is well known. He is referred to by name in Sartre's short story *L'Enfance d'un chef* [*The Childhood of a Leader*] (French pub. 1939).—TRANS.

109. In his preface to *Vies imaginaires* (Paris: G. Crès, 1921).

110. "The poet is comparable to the king of the clouds." Baudelaire, "L'Albatros" ["The Albatross"], *Les Fleurs du mal* [*Flowers of Evil*], *Oeuvres complètes*.

111. The expression is Mallarmé's. See *Cantique de Saint Jean* [*The Canticle of Saint John*], *Oeuvres complètes*, 49.

112. *Hérodiade, Oeuvres complètes*, 47.

113. "I only believe in two kinds of distinction, both equally chimerical. The first stems from the delirium of a people for whom art furnishes new idols; the second comes from seeing oneself in a much-admired book, placed there by the author's unwitting intention." Letter by Mallarmé to J.-K. Huysmans, 18 May 1884. Mondor, *Vie*, 433.

114. ". . . To endow (things) with splendor, through empty space, with endless solitary feasts." Mallarmé, "La Musique et les lettres," *Oeuvres complètes*, 647.

115. Cf. "Epilogue III," *Poèmes saturniens*.

116. If nothing exists but thou, Hari, O Supreme God!

. . . . . . . . . . . . . . . . . . . . . . . . . . . . . . . . . . . . . . . . . . . . . . . . . . . . . . . . . . . . . . .

Why is it that, flooding the world with tears
You suffer so, My Master, in the depths of the human soul?

[S'il n'est rien, sinon toi, Hâri, suprême Dieu!

. . . . . . . . . . . . . . . . . . . . . . . . . . . . . . . . . . . . . . . . . . . . . . . . . . . . . . . . . . . . . . .

D'où vient que, remplissant la terre de sanglots,
Tu souffres, ô mon Maître, au sein de l'âme humaine?]
    Leconte de Lisle, "La Vision de Brahma," *Poèmes antiques*

117. Sartre's italics.

118. From the draft of a letter of 1865 to Jules Janin, the literary critic and novelist. Cf. Baudelaire, *Oeuvres complètes*, vol. II.

119. Letter from Mallarmé to Cazalis, 3 June 1863. Mondor, *Vie*, 92.

120. Letter from Cazalis to Mallarmé. Mondor, *Vie*.

121. Sartre probably meant "existence."

122. This is undoubtedly an allusion to a line by Mallarmé. The latter (according to Mondor), at the instigation of Catulle Mendès, sought to establish a poets' chapel in 1873, at which time he wrote to Mistral: "We should be ashamed of ourselves! All we basically want is to take a head count, rub shoulders, ensure that works by absentees are read and that those who put in an appearance take note of one another." From a letter of 1 November 1873. Mondor, *Vie*, 352.

123. The reference is to Marx. Cf. *The German Ideology*, Part 1, "Theses on Feuerbach."


## II. THE CHOSEN ONE

### 1. A Phantom Marriage

124. The translator claims full responsibility for this subheading, as well as for the one on page 79.—Trans.

125. Mondor, *Vie*.

126. Letter to J.-M. Heredia, 22 June 1871. Mondor, *Vie*, 320.

127. The reference is to *Igitur*. This reading, according to Mondor, took place in 1870. *Vie*, 301.

128. C. Mendès, *Rapport sur le mouvement poétique français de 1867 à 1900*.

129. Le Parnasse Contemporain, "a collection of new poetry" which appeared in three volumes published by Lemerre over a period of ten years (1866; 1869–71; 1876), represented, at its apogee, the works of fifty-six poets all writing in the vein of Parnassian realism.—Trans.

130. Théodore de Banville's advice refers to *Hérodiade*, then under consideration for possible performance by the Théâtre Français.

131. The allusion is to Baudelaire's "L'Albatros":

The poet is kin to that Prince of the cloudy hall
Who haunts the tempest and sneers at the archer's call
Exiled on land midst hisses of all
His giant wings make him stumble and fall.

[Le poète est semblable au prince des nuées
Qui hante la templête et se rit de l'archer;
Exilé sur le sol au milieu des huées,
Ses ailes de géant l'empêchent de marcher.]

132. Cf. "Le Guignon." Mallarmé, *Oeuvres complètes*, 29.

133. This composite quotation, derived from several sources, expresses a grievance which reappears frequently in the poet's correspondence of the 1860s. See, e.g., Mallarmé's letter to Cazalis, February 1865; see also *Igitur*, *Oeuvres complètes*, 440.

134. Letter to Cazalis, 23 March 1864. Mondor, *Vie*.

135. Letter to Cazalis, 4 April 1862. Mondor, *Vie*, 56.

136. Mallarmé's comment about a forlorn young girl was related by Henri de Régnier. Mondor, *Vie*.

137. Letter from Mallarmé to Cazalis, 4 April 1862. Mondor, *Vie*, 56.

138. Valmont and Samuel Cramer are, respectively, the protagonists of Laclos's *Les Liaisons dangereuses* [*Dangerous Encounters*] and of Baudelaire's "Fanfarlo."

139. Verlaine, "Voeu" ["Vow"], *Poèmes saturniens*.

140. Verlaine, "Lassitude," *Poèmes saturniens*.

141. Verlaine, "Mon rêve familier" ["My Familiar Dream"], *Poèmes saturniens*.

142. "Was it not you, my sister with an olden look, who sought the words 'the grace of faded things' in one of my poems? You also have no taste for new things, whose vulgarity alarms you, and still you cannot refuse them—an awkward position for those with no taste for action."
Mallarmé, "Frisson d'hiver" ["Winter Shiver"], *Poèmes en prose*, *Oeuvres complètes*, 272.

143. Verlaine, "Lassitude," *Poèmes saturniens*.

144. Octave Mirbeau (1848–1917), the novelist and critic who was also the dominant representative of bourgeois theater under the Third Republic, was best known for his comedy *Les Affaires sont les affaires* [*Business Is Business*], 1903.—TRANS.

145. Michel Leiris (b. 1901), the ethnographer who is best known for this unsparing and disabused autobiography *L'Age d'homme* [*Manhood*] (French pub. 1939).—TRANS.

146. Cf. Verlaine, "Mon rêve familier," *Poèmes saturniens*.

147. From an 1862 letter to Cazalis. Mondor, *Vie*.

148. Letter to Cazalis, 23 March 1864. At this time, Mallarmé was twenty-two years old. Mondor, *Vie*.

149. Eugène Lefébure.

150. Letter to Cazalis, 9 December 1863. Mondor, *Vie*, 101.

151. Letter to Cazalis, 10 August 1866. Mondor, *Vie*, 218

152. Letter to Mistral, 30 December 1864. Mondor, *Vie*, 149.

153. Letter to Aubanel, 27 November 1864. Mondor, *Vie*, 150.
154. Letter to Cazalis. Mondor, *Vie*.
155. Letter to Cazalis, 26 December 1864. Mondor, *Vie*, 150–51.
156. Letter to Méry Laurent, 1889.
157. Letter to Cazalis, 7 January 1869. Mondor, *Vie*, 276.
158. "To hear within me the melody of certain mysterious sounds, I need to feel inner peace and my mind must be *entirely unencumbered by memories*." From a letter to the Provençal poet Théodore Aubanel, December 1865. Mondor, *Vie*, 179.
159. "Nature was the first tangible Idea to give my blurred senses a hint of reality and, as direct compensation, to fire my youth with an intensity which I could just as well call passion." "Bucolique," *Variations sur un sujet*, *Oeuvres complètes*, 402.
160. "Bucolique," *Oeuvres complètes*, 402.
161. Mallarmé, "Plainte d'automne" ["Autumn Complaint"], *Poèmes en prose*, *Oeuvres complètes*, 270.
162. Ibid.
163. "Un soir d'octobre, Premier vers" ["An October Evening, First Line"]; cf. Verlaine, *Oeuvres Poétiques complètes* (Paris: Gallimard, Bibliothèque de la Pléiade, 1938).
164. Verlaine, "Crépuscule du soir mystique" ["Mystic Evening Twilight"], *Poèmes saturniens*.
165. Letter from Lefébure to Mallarmé, 9 May 1866. Mondor, *Eugène Lefébure*, 217.
166. Letters to Cazalis and to Aubanel, December 1865. Mondor, *Vie*.
167. "In this world a poet can only be a poet, but I am a walking dead man, a mere shadow of myself. I even doubt that I might one day make a claim to the title of amateur." Letter to Cazalis, November 1864. Mondor, *Vie*, 150.
168. Mondor, *Vie*.

## 2. The Dead Hand of the Past

169. "Autobiographie," *Oeuvres complètes*, 661.
170. Etienne (Stéphane) Mallarmé was born on 18 March 1842.
171. "I bear you a child of an Idumaean night!" The first line of "Don du poème" ["The Bestowal of the Poem"], *Poésies*, *Oeuvres complètes*, 40.
172. "Autobiographie," *Oeuvres complètes*, 661.
173. "Eventail" ["Fan"], *Poésies*, *Oeuvres complètes*, 58.
174. Cf. Baudelaire, "Moesta et errabunda," *Les Fleurs du mal*, *Oeuvres complètes*.
175. Eugène and Jacques Crépet, Baudelaire's biographers and editors.
176. Jules Buisson, a childhood friend of Baudelaire.
177. Charles Mauron, in his preface to *Mallarmé l'obscur* (Paris: Denoël, 1941). Mondor, *Mallarmé plus intime*.
178. Sartre is quoting the critic André Rousseaux discussing "the great current of supernatural eroticism [that swept the century]." Mondor, *Mallarmé plus intime*.
179. Verlaine's *Poèmes saturniens* (1866) show the preponderant influence of Hugo, Baudelaire, and the Parnassians on the poet, who had not yet perfected his gentle, incantatory style.—TRANS.
180. *Introduction à la psychanalyse de Mallarmé* (Neuchâtel: La Baconnière, 1950).
181. Charles Mauron, known for his "psychocritical" interpretations of major literary figures whose "obsessive themes" became his privileged object of analysis,

published his *Introduction à la psychanalyse de Mallarmé* in 1950, two years prior to the present work.—TRANS.

182. *The German Ideology*, Part 1.

183. "Sa fosse est creusée! . . ." ["Her Grave Is Dug! . . ."], II, *Poèmes d'enfance et de jeunesse, Oeuvres complètes*, 6.

184. "Sa fosse est fermée . . ." ["Her Grave Is Sealed . . ."], *Oeuvres complètes*, 7.

185. Cf. *Igitur, Oeuvres complètes*, 435.

186. Letter to Mistral, 31 December 1865. Mondor, *Vie*.

187. This expression by Mallarmé's friend Lefébure appears in a letter of 16 December 1867. Mondor, *Eugène Lefébure*, 281.

188. Cf. "Las de l'amer repos" ["Weary of this bitter rest"], *Poésies, Oeuvres complètes*, 35.

189. Cf. "Don du Poème," *Oeuvres complètes*, 40.

190. Cf. "Toast funèbre" ["Funeral Toast"], *Oeuvres complètes*, 55.

191. "Toast funèbre," *Oeuvres complètes*, 55.

192. Cf. "Le Nénuphar blanc" ["The White Water-Lily"], *Poèmes en prose, Oeuvres complètes*, 284.

193. Cf. "La Musique et les lettres," *Oeuvres complètes*, 647.

194. Cf. "Une dentelle s'abolit" ["A Piece of Lace Abolishes Itself"], *Poésies, Oeuvres complètes*, 74:

> But in him who gilds his dreams
> Sadly sleeps a mandora
> Musician with a hollow void
>
> [Mais, chez qui du rêve se dore
> Tristement dort une mandore
> Au creux néant musicien]

195. A character whom André Gide fashioned after Oscar Wilde in *L'Immoraliste* [*The Immoralist*].

196. *L'Après-midi d'un faune* [*The Afternoon of a Faun*], *Poésies, Oeuvres complètes*, 50.

197. "What pain also agonizes the Chimera whose seeping wounds of gold bear witness to the equality of all being." "La Musique et les Lettres," *Oeuvres complètes*, 647.

198. *L'Après-midi d'un faune, Oeuvres complètes*, 50.

199. "Enslaved to absolute rule, we know that nothing is but what is." "La Musique et les Lettres," *Oeuvres complètes*, 647.

200. Cf. "Sur l'Idéal à vingt ans" ["On What Is Ideal at Twenty"], *Oeuvres complètes*, 883.

201. Cf. "La Musique et les Lettres," *Oeuvres complètes*, 647, and "Crise de vers" ["The Crisis in Poetry"], *Variations sur un sujet, Oeuvres complètes*, 368.

202. His grandfather's authority would supplant the diminishing influence of his remarried father, who later would turn impotent.

203. Cf. "Quant au livre," *Variations sur un sujet, Oeuvres complètes*, 372.

204. In this description of the monotony of bureaucratic existence, Sartre is indebted to Heidegger's description of *Alltäglichkeit*, the drab reality of routine life where stale ideas and emotions felt by people are interchangeable.—TRANS.

205. Cf. *Igitur, Oeuvres complètes*, 440: "He wrests himself free from indefinite

time and comes alive! And now no longer does time move as it once did, when, with a dull shiver, it came to rest on massive ebony trees whose illusions sealed the lips with an overwhelming sensation that it's all over."

206. Letter to Cazalis, 5 August 1867. Mondor, *Vie*, 244.

207. "Pauvre enfant pâle" ["O Pitiable Pale Child"], *Poèmes en prose, Oeuvres complètes*, 274.

208. Cf. "La fausse entrée des sorcières dans *Macbeth*" ["The Witches' False Entrance in *Macbeth*"], *Crayonné au théâtre [Theater Sketches], Oeuvres complètes*, 348.

209. "Le Guignon" (first version), *Premiers poèmes, Oeuvres complètes*, 1411.

210. Letter from Mme. Desmolins. Mondor, *Vie*.

211. Mondor, *Vie*.

212. Ibid.

213. 24 August 1860. Mondor, *Vie*, 21.

214. 18 November 1860. Mondor, *Vie*, 22.

215. "Autobiographie," *Oeuvres complètes*, 662.

216. Letter to Cazalis, 1 April 1863. Mondor, *Vie*, 85.

217. At that time Mallarmé's grandfather urged young Stéphane to pursue the family career. The correspondence between grandfather and grandson was published by Mondor in *Mallarmé plus intime*.

218. Letter to Aubanel, 31 December 1865. Mondor, *Vie*, 185.

219. "Toast funèbre," *Poésies, Oeuvres complètes*.

220. The reference is to the protagonist of Mallarmé's work by the same name.

221. Letter to Cazalis, 4 June 1862. Mondor, *Vie*, 51.

222. Letter to Cazalis, 1 April 1863. Mondor, *Vie*.

223. "L'Orphelin" ["The Orphan"], first version, *Oeuvres complètes*, 1559.

224. Mallarmé dedicated two poems to Alfred Espinas: "Pépita" and "Mélancolie." *Oeuvres complètes*, 1384.

225. Letter to Cazalis, 24 July 1863.

226. Ibid.

227. Ibid.

228. Mondor, *Mallarmé plus intime*.

229. The reference is to the two children's stepmother.

230. Letter to Maria, May 1857. Mondor, *Mallarmé plus intime*, 72.

231. Cf. Verlaine, "Epilogue III," *Poèmes saturniens, Oeuvres complètes*.

232. "An insignificant rumble to bruit about the empty act." Cf. *Un coup de dés . . .*

233. "Le Nénuphar blanc," *Poèmes en prose, Oeuvres complètes*, 286.

234. Cf. Baudelaire, "Mon coeur mis à nu," *Oeuvres complètes*.

235. Letter to Lefébure, 17 May 1867. Mondor, *Eugène Lefébure*, 351. [Cf. note 39, page 34.—Trans.]

236. The expression appears in "Le Pitre châtié" ["The Chastized Clown"]. *Poésies, Oeuvres complètes*, 31. The word "châtié" may also be translated as "refined" or "polished"—an ambiguity lost in English translation.—Trans.

237. The allusion is to the hero of Schiller's drama *Die Räuber*. See note 30, page 31.

238. At this point Sartre's text becomes fragmentary. Since no manuscript version of these pages exists, the arrangement in *Obliques* is followed. The reader may detect some repetitions in the forthcoming pages, such as Sartre's treatment of Mallarmé's relationship to his father, which he now examines in significantly greater depth. We assume that Sartre's outline was not definitive.

239. Cf. page 47, note 72.

240. *Igitur*, critical notes, *Oeuvres complètes*, 450.

241. "I experience no fulfillment, but I live surrounded by beauty." In "Symphonie Littéraire" ["Literary Symphony"], *Proses de jeunesse, Oeuvres complètes*, 262.

242. There is a possible misreading of the word *glissement (rongeur)* in *Obliques* (here translated as "scratching"—TRANS.). An earlier manuscript version of this sentence reads: "I don't know the meaning of joy, the child will say. Somewhat later, he will even outdo Baudelaire when he decides to embrace the neurotic cult of "voluptuousness," with its sterile delights marked by total negativity, like a diamond screaking (*crissement*) the windowpane which separates him from the world."

243. Reported by Mme. Desmolins, maternal grandmother of the two children, in a letter to another family member, 2 November 1852. Mondor, *Vie*, 14.

244. Mondor, *Vie*, 14.

245. "L'Orphelin," first version of "Réminiscence." Cf. *Oeuvres complètes*, 1559 and 278.

246. The poet's son, who died in 1879 at the age of eight.

247. The publication of Mallarmé's complete correspondence was initiated in 1959 by Editions Gallimard, which recently brought out the final volume. Since in it Mallarmé's half-sisters are barely mentioned, it is difficult to get at the poet's real feelings toward the various members of his family. A letter to his oldest half-sister, Jeanne, written in 1873 on the occasion of her marriage, might be considered affectionate were it not replete with the florid conventions typical of French correspondence.

248. From a letter written by Mallarmé's maternal grandmother in 1864, announcing to her cousin the birth of Geneviève, Mallarmé's daughter: "May this dear little girl inherit her poor grandmother's virtues rather than the vivid imagination which wore her out." Mondor, *Vie*, 148.

249. Here Sartre is taking mental note, for purposes of future commentary, of the Double Postulation theme in Mallarmé's quatrain (1874) based on Manet's lithograph, *Polichinelle:*

> Polichinelle dances with his double hunched back,
> One hunch points down and the other up high,
> His just soul inspired by these double desires,
> See how forever he falls and he rises!

> [Polichinelle danse avec deux bosses, mais
> L'une vise le sol et l'autre l'Empyrée,
> Par ce double désir âme juste inspirée,
> Vois-le qui toujours tombe et surgit à jamais!]
> (*Vers de circonstance, Oeuvres complètes*, 161).

250. "In every man and at all times there are two simultaneous postulations which embrace either God or Satan. The appeal to God, or spirituality, shows a desire for self-improvement; the appeal to Satan, or bestiality, on the other hand, represents our natural propensity for self-degradation. Love of women and intimate relations with animals, dogs, cats, etc., should be considered a manifestation of the latter." Baudelaire, "Mon coeur mis à nu," *Oeuvres complètes*, 1277.

251. "*Surgi de la croupe et du bond*" ["*Begot of Rump and Romp*"], *Poésies, Oeuvres complètes*, 74.

252. The double postulation is also present in Corbière. Cf. "Le Rénégat" ["The Renegade"], *Les Amours jaunes:*

He killed every *beast,* warded off every blow . . .
Purified by purging every trace of disgust.

[Il a tué toute *bête,* éreinté tous les coups . . .
Pur à force d'avoir purgé tous les dégoûts.]

See also "Femme" ["Woman"], *Les Amours jaunes:* "Once the *bestial* lust which draws woman toward man has been quenched, woman aspires to beauty.—A sleepless night . . . a foul day . . ."

253. Cf. "Placet futile," *Poésies, Oeuvres complètes,* 30:

Princess! Because to Hebe's fortune I aspire
Which marks this cup by the touch of your lips,
I expire from desire though merely a squire . . .

[Princesse! à jalouser le destin d'une Hébé
Qui poind sur cette tasse au baiser de vos lèvres,
J'use de mes feux mais n'ai rang discret que d'abbé . . .]

In Greek mythology, the daughter of Zeus and Hera. To the Romans she was known as Juventa and became known as the patron saint of young manhood. This playful sample of Mallarmé's verbal artistry is an extreme case of the sign pointing "to itself and not to something else" (Todorov)—TRANS.

254. Paul Bourget (1852–1935), whose novel *Le Disciple* (1889) championed the nuclear family and traditional Christian values. He was influenced by Frédéric Le Play (1806–82), a foe of socialist and liberal doctrine who, in matters of Church and State, espoused an authoritarian position garbed in paternalism.—TRANS.

255. In *Les Nourritures terrestres* (1897).

256. At this juncture there is a break in the *Obliques* text. The ensuing lines within brackets appear at the bottom of a page from a previous handwritten draft. In all likelihood Sartre forgot to recopy them. After commenting on the social and historical aspects of the failure of the family, Sartre returns to his discussion of Mallarmé's particular style of revolt.

257. "Une dentelle s'abolit," *Poésies, Oeuvres complètes,* 74.

258. "Les Fenêtres" ["Windows"], *Poésies, Oeuvres complètes,* 33.

259. "Villiers de l'Isle-Adam," *Oeuvres complètes,* 481.

260. Letter from Mallarmé to Cazalis, March 1865. Mondor, *Vie,* 160–61.

261. Letter to Cazalis, November 1864. Mondor, *Vie,* 150.

262. Compare, e.g., Mallarmé's "Les Fleurs" ["Flowers"], in *Poésies, Oeuvres complètes,* 33, with this line from Victor Hugo in "La Légende des siècles" ["The Legend of the Centuries"]:

Avalanches of gold flooded the azure, skies

[Des avalanches d'or s'inondaient dans l'azur]

[Cf. Mondor, *Vie,* 119, note 2.—TRANS.]

263. Mallarmé, *Poésies, Oeuvres complètes,* 30:

> . . . Passed, ever letting fall from her unclenched hands
> Snow-white bouquets of fragrant stars.
>
> [ . . . Passait, laissant toujours de ses mains mal fermées
> Neiger de blancs bouquets d'étoiles parfumées.]

Compare with these lines from Hugo's "Chants du crépuscule" ["Evening Song"]:

> . . . Through the fingers of your unclenched hands
> All earthly goods glimmer in fragrant clusters.
>
> [ . . . Luire à travers les doigts de tes mains mal fermées
> Tous les biens de ce monde en grappes parfumées.]

264. Cf. "Le Guignon," *Poésies, Oeuvres complètes.*
265. Cf. "Symphonie littéraire," *Oeuvres complètes,* 261.
266. Ibid.
267. In 1948 *Les Lettres* published this dialogue for the first time (nos. 9, 10, and 11). There are also two nymphs in *Diane au bois,* a verse play by Théodore de Banville first performed in 1863. The satyr Gnifron, like Mallarmé's Faun, yearns for both the brunette and the blonde. Certain aspects of Hérodiade also recall Banville's Diane.
268. "Conflit" ["Conflict"], *Variations sur un sujet, Oeuvres complètes,* 355.
269. Cf. "In Memoriam, Stéphane Mallarmé (1898)," *Prétextes* (Paris: Mercure de France, 1913).
270. Villiers de l'Isle-Adam, *Premières poésies, Oeuvres complètes* (Geneva: Slatkine Reprints, 1970; first French pub. 1859).
271. Cf. "Toast funèbre," *Poésies, Oeuvres complètes,* 55.
272. Ibid., 56.
273. Mallarmé, "Villiers de l'Isle-Adam," *Oeuvres complètes,* 481.
274. The game is played by translating Mallarmé's imperatives into Kantian categories.
275. Letter to Cazalis, 1862. Mondor, *Vie.*
276. Letter to Cazalis, October 1864. Mallarmé's italics. Mondor, *Vie,* 145.
277. Letter to Cazalis, 14 May 1867. Mondor, *Vie.*
278. Cf. page 115, note 268.
279. Letter to Cazalis, June 1865. Mondor, *Vie,* 166.
280. "My total involvement with *Hérodiade,* the source of all my doubts and tribulations, at last allowed me to find the subtle words I sought." Letter to Cazalis, July 1866. Mondor, *Vie,* 211.
281. Cf. Letter to Cazalis, 14 May 1867: "Now I have become detached, and instead of the Stéphane you once knew, I have developed a talent derived from the spiritual realm for seeing and transforming my old self." Mondor, *Vie,* 237.
282. Letter to Cazalis, 14 May 1867. Mondor, *Vie,* 237.
283. Letter to Cazalis, April 1866. Mondor, *Vie.*
284. Ibid.
285. Letter to Lefébure, 17 May 1867. Mondor, *Eugène Lefébure,* 354.

286. In your heart a moonbeam slumbers,
     O sweet beam of summer light,
     Away from life which so encumbers
     Neath your glow might I sink into night.

     [Dans ton coeur dort un clair de lune,
     Un doux clair de lune d'été,
     Et loin de la vie importune
     Je me veux perdre en ta clarté.]
        Jean Lahor, "Chanson triste," *L'Illusion* (Paris: Alphonse Lemerre, 1875–93)
287. Letter from Cazalis to Mallarmé. Mondor, *Vie.*
288. Letter from Lefébure to Mallarmé, 16 February 1865. Mondor, *Eugène Lefébure,* 187.
289. Villiers de l'Isle-Adam, *Axêl.* Cf. Mallarmé, *Oeuvres complètes,* 505.
290. Letter from Lefébure to Mallarmé, 15 July 1866. Mondor, *Eugène Lefébure.*
291. Oh, God! Eventide, by your bitter spring
     I saw the bareness of my slender dream!

     [Mais, horreur! des soirs, dans ta sévère fontaine,
     J'ai de mon rêve épars connu la nudité!]
                *Hérodiade, Oeuvres complètes,* 45
292. "Quant au livre," *Oeuvres complètes,* 369.
293. In a letter to Lefébure of 17 May 1867, Mallarmé writes: "Each birth is ruinous, and at each moment of life we agonize over what we have unwittingly lost." Mondor, *Eugène Lefébure,* 352.
294. Cf. letter to François Coppée, 5 December 1866. Mondor, *Vie.*
295. Cf. "Crise de vers," *Oeuvres complètes,* 367.
296. Letter to Lefébure, 3 May 1868. Mondor, *Vie.*
297. Or rather, "of delicate stature." Cf. *Un coup de dés . . ., Oeuvres complètes,* 470. The new character is the protagonist of *Igitur,* which the poet composed between 1867 and 1870.
298. A break in the continuity of the text occurs at this point. The scattered words within brackets come from a fragment written prior to this passage and probably provide only a part of the missing text.
     It is through *Igitur,* whose subtitle is *The Madness of Elbehnon,* that Mallarmé's personal crisis rises to the level of an "ontological drama"; the missing passage probably would have announced this drama.
299. "Villiers de l'Isle-Adam," *Oeuvres complètes.*
300. To compare Sartre's own conception of creativity with that of Mallarmé's, see Sartre's *Cahiers pour une morale,* esp. 457 et seq.
301. "La Musique et les Lettres," *Oeuvres complètes,* 647.
302. Self-identical space, waxing or waning
     Wallows in the boredom of those vile luminaries who swear
     That genius was sparked by a festive star.

     [L'espace à soi pareil qu'il s'accroisse ou se nie
     Roule dans cet ennui des feux vils pour témoins
     Que s'est d'un astre en fête allumé le génie.]
                "Plusieurs sonnets," *Poésies, Oeuvres complètes,* 67

303. If, thanks to him, one blows his grotesque tin horn,
Children will wrench us into stubborn laughter . . .

[Grâce à lui, si l'un souffle à son buccin bizarre,
Des enfants nous tordront en un rire obstiné . . .]
"Le Guignon," *Poésies, Oeuvres complètes,* 29
304. Letter to Cazalis, 14 May 1867. Mondor, *Vie,* 237.
305. Cf. *Un coup de dés . . ., Oeuvres complètes,* 464.
306. "La Cour" ["The Court"], *Variations sur un sujet, Oeuvres complètes,* 414.
307. Letter to Cazalis, 14 May 1867. Mondor, *Vie,* 237.
[In this dialecticized passage, with its direct reference to the Hegelian Unhappy Consciousness and its indirect one to his World-Historical Individual, Sartre turns to Hegel's *Phenomenology* as a compass to indicate the directions of the maturing poet's inner landscape.—TRANS.]
308. Letter to Lefébure, 17 May 1867. Mondor, *Eugène Lefébure,* 349.
309. "La Cour," *Variations sur un sujet, Oeuvres complètes,* 414.
310. Cf. page 114, note 262.
311. *Igitur,* notes, *Oeuvres complètes,* 428.
312. *Igitur,* critical notes, *Oeuvres complètes,* 451.
313. Ibid.
314. *Igitur, Oeuvres complètes,* 441.
315. *Crayonné au théâtre (Theater Sketches), Oeuvres complètes,* 300.
316. "Yes, *I know,* we are nothing but vain configurations of matter—yet sufficiently sublime to have invented God and Soul. In fact, so very sublime, my friend, that I want to give myself the pleasure of beholding self-conscious matter rushing madly about in this non-existent dream of ours." Letter to Cazalis, March 1866. Mondor, *Vie,* 193.
317. Cf. *Un coup de dés . . ., Oeuvres complètes,* 461.
318. Cf. *Igitur, Oeuvres complètes,* 434.
319. Letter from Mallarmé to Lefébure, 17 May 1867. Mondor, *Eugène Lefébure,* 349.
320. Letter to Lefébure, 17 May 1867. Mondor, *Eugène Lefébure,* 349. Mallarmé's italics.
321. *Igitur, Oeuvres complètes,* 434.
322. "Age-old race, for whom the weight of time is lifted. So great was it in former times and so laden with contingency, that it could only live for the future." *Iqitur, Oeuvres complètes,* 442.
323. *Igitur, Oeuvres complètes,* 440.
324. *Igitur,* critical notes, *Oeuvres complètes,* 450.
325. Letter from Mallarmé to Lefébure, 17 May 1867. Mondor, *Eugène Lefébure,* 348. Mallarmé's italics.
326. Mondor, *Eugène Lefébure,* 349.
327. Mallarmé's words. Cf. "Hamlet," *Crayonné au théâtre (Theater Sketches), Oeuvres complètes,* 302.
328. Cf. *Igitur, Oeuvres complètes,* 442.
329. Letter to Cazalis, 14 May 1867. Mondor, *Vie,* 237.
330. Victoriously eluded sweet suicide
Firebrand of glory, froth of blood, gold, tempest!

[Victorieusement fui le suicide beau
Tison de gloire, sang par écume, or, tempête!]
"Plusieurs sonnets," III, *Oeuvres complètes*, 68

331. Cf. "La fausse entrée des sorcières dans *Macbeth*," *Crayonné au théâtre, Oeuvres complètes*, 348.

332. Mondor, *Vie*.

333. *Igitur*, critical notes, *Oeuvres complètes*, 451.

334. Ibid.

335. *Igitur*, "Argument," *Oeuvres complètes*, 434.

336. Letter to Cazalis, April 1866. Mondor, *Vie*.

337. "This is the outline for my lyrical volume whose title might be *Glorious Lies* or *Glorified Lies*. I will sing out of desperation." Mondor, *Vie*.

338. "La Musique et les Lettres," *Oeuvres complètes*, 645.

339. *Les Mots anglais* [*English Words*], *Oeuvres complètes*, 901.

340. "I have been rescued from death by the precious key which opens my last spiritual coffer. Now that there exist no more secondhand impressions, it is my turn to open it, and its secret will turn into a beautiful sky." Letter to Aubanel, 16 July 1866. Mondor, *Vie*, 212.

341. Henri Regnault, the promising young painter who was killed in his twenty-eighth year at the battle of Buzenval.

342. Letter to Cazalis, 23 April 1871. Mondor, *Vie*, 313.

343. Letter to Odilon Redon, 18 February 1885. Mondor, *Vie*, 453. Mallarmé's italics.

344. Frozen he faces the cold dream of scorn
With which the swan cloaks itself in its futile exile.

[Il s'immobilise au songe froid de mépris
Que vêt parmi l'exil inutile le Cygne.]
"Plusieurs sonnets," II, *Poésies, Oeuvres complètes*, 68

345. "La Musique et les Lettres," *Oeuvres complètes*, 647.

346. Nothing, this foam, this virgin verse
Designating only the cup . . .

[Rien, cette écume, vierge vers
A ne désigner que la coupe . . .]

347. *La Phénoménologie de l'esprit* [*Phenomenology of Mind*], vol. I (Paris: Editions Aubier, 1947), 171.

[Quoted by Jean Hyppolite in *Genèse et structure de la* Phénoménologie de l'esprit *de Hegel*, 177. (Paris: Editions Montaigne, 1946). Sartre apparently turned to his open copy of Hyppolite's influential commentary on the *Phenomenology* when he cited this and other passages from Hegel.—TRANS.]

348. *La Phénoménologie de l'esprit*, vol. I, 171.


## III. REQUIEM FOR A POET:

349. Cf. page 102, note 207.

350. Cf. page 113, note 259.

351. Cf. *Igitur, Oeuvres complètes*, 436 et seq.

352. "Plusieurs sonnets," I, *Oeuvres complètes*, 67.

353. *Igitur*, notes, *Oeuvres complètes*, 428.

354. *Igitur*, critical notes, *Oeuvres complètes*, 451.

355. "Hamlet," *Crayonné au théâtre*, *Oeuvres complètes*, 300.

356. "Villiers de l'Isle-Adam," *Oeuvres complètes*, 481.

357. Cf. page 121, note 301.

358. In the sense of a "flawed product."

359. Cities in which Mallarmé was employed as an English teacher.

360. Flaubert's, *La Tentation de Saint Antoine* (1848–74).

361. Cf. page 127, note 331.

362. Cf. page 128, note 335.

363. Cf. page 121, note 295.

364. Cf. page 131, note 348.

365. Cf. *Igitur*, critical notes, *Oeuvres complètes*, 450: "A spiral, on whose summit he was perched, omnipotent, immobilized."

366. Maurice Blanchot, *Faux pas* (Paris: Gallimard, 1943).

367. Cf. page 126, Mallarmé's text and note 325.

368. "The only kind of bomb I know is a book." Mondor, *Vie*. See also the interview with Mallarmé in the 27 May 1894 edition of *Le Soir*, regarding the young anarchist Félix Fénéon, in *Correspondence*, vol. VI.

369. The following passage within brackets was never edited. It was undoubtedly included in the manuscript version of the article submitted to the original editor. It could be argued that Sartre deleted it from the proofs because he found it unsatisfactory, although it is rather more likely that Raymond Queneau, under editorial pressure, asked Sartre to remove it; in any event, it is the only passage which could be excluded from the text without distorting it. After showing *why* the poet's final project could only be the suicidal poem, Sartre carefully analyzes *how* Mallarmé dealt with language by baring the techniques he employed to effect his goals.

370. "The pure work implies the elocutionary disappearance of the poet, who lets words, which are chosen for their clashing inequalities, 'do their own thing.' " "Crise de vers," *Variations sur un sujet*, *Oeuvres complètes*, 366.

371. More precisely: "They take light from mutual reflection, like an actual trail of fire (over precious stones) . . ." This is a continuation of the prior quote. Cf. "Le Mystère dans les Lettres" ["The Mystery in Letters"], *Oeuvres complètes*, 386: "Words all tend to take light from mutual reflection."

372. "Crise de vers," *Oeuvres complètes*, 367, and "La Musique et les Lettres," *Oeuvres complètes*, 647.

373. Mallarmé's expression, in a letter to André Gide, 14 May 1897, where the typographic layout of *Un coup de dés* is discussed. *Oeuvres complètes*, 1582.

374. Cf. Paul Valéry, *Eupalinos ou l'Architecte* (Paris: Gallimard, 1944; first published 1921).

375. In a letter from Mallarmé to the Belgian poet Georges Rodenbach, 25 March 1888, on his book of poems *Du silence*. Cf. *L'Amitié de Stéphane Mallarmé et de Georges Rodenbach* [*The Friendship Betwen Stéphane Mallarmé and Georges Rodenbach*] (Geneva: P. Cailler, 1949) and *Correspondance de Mallarmé*.

376. Cf. page 96, note 201.

377. "Victorieusement fui le suicide beau" ["Triumphantly Fled Sweet Suicide"], *Poésies*, *Oeuvres complètes*, 68.

378. Letter to G. Rodenbach. Cf. our note 350, p. 186.

379. Cf. letter from Mallarmé to F. Vielé-Griffin, 8 August 1891. Mondor, *Vie*, 616.

380. Cf. page 101, note 206.

381. Poulet, *Espace et temps*.

382. *Un coup de dés . . ., Oeuvres complètes*, 474, 475.

383. "Autres poèmes et sonnets" ["Other Poems and Sonnets"], *Poésies, Oeuvres complètes*, 74.

384. "Hommages et tombeaux" ["Tributes and Memorials"], *Oeuvres complètes*, 69.

385. "Plusieurs sonnets," II, *Oeuvres complètes*, 67.

386. Ibid., 68.

387. Cf. page 93, note 193.

388. Cf. *Igitur, Oeuvres complètes*, 441.

389. "But I adore our conscious use of tricks to project our shortcomings onto forbidden, thunderstruck heights, where they are blown away." "La Musique et les Lettres," *Oeuvres complètes*, 647.

390. Cf. "Autobiographie," *Oeuvres complètes*, 663.

391. Cf. "Villiers de l'Isle-Adam," *Oeuvres complètes*, 495.

392. Cf. "Hamlet," *Crayonné au théâtre, Oeuvres complètes*, 300, 302.

393. In the poet's last wishes: ". . . Burn, then. No, my poor children, there is no literary legacy here. . . . Believe me, it was meant to be very beautiful." Mondor, *Vie*, 804.

394. "In front of his sheet of paper, the artist *creates himself*." Mallarmé in a letter to Lefébure, 1865. Mondor, *Eugène Lefébure*.

395. The expression is Mallarmé's. Cf. "Sur l'Idéal à vingt ans," *Oeuvres complètes*, 883.

396. Cf. quotation and note 379, page 141.

397. I, sylph of this cold ceiling!
     "Surgi de la croupe et du bond,"
          *Poésies, Oeuvres complètes*, 74

398. "But my full admiration goes out to the great, unconsolable Wizard, relentless seeker of a mystery he knows does not exist, yet one he will seek endlessly from the mournful depths of his lucid despair, because it *might have been* the Truth." Letter to Odilon Redon, 18 February 1885. Mondor, *Vie*, 453. [Cf. note 343, page 130.—TRANS.]

# Index

# MALLARMÉ

## OR THE POET OF NOTHINGNESS

*Jean-Paul Sartre*

*Translated and Introduced by Ernest Sturm*

At first glance, one would be hard put to find two more disparate personalities: Jean-Paul Sartre, the philosopher of *commitment*, and Mallarmé, the poet of *detachment*; Sartre, the flamboyant and irreverent intellectual whose restless curiosity did not know the meaning of restraint and whose pen was always on the move, and Mallarmé, the cramped and prissy eccentric who looked to poetry as his only path to salvation, all the while grumbling that he had nothing to say and nothing with which to say it.

Yet despite such differences, Sartre hailed Mallarmé as a "hero, prophet, wizard and tragedian"—the "herald" of our century and "the greatest of our poets."

When Sartre wrote the present study in 1953, at the height of his intellectual powers, his commitment to Mallarmé was total. For many years his manuscript had been missing. Only recently was it rediscovered and made available to the French reading public.

*Mallarmé, or the Poet of Nothingness*, a translation which was four years in the making, now brings this unusual and rich work to the English-speaking reader. As a biographical study, it casts a provocative spell and ranks, in depth if not in length, with Sartre's other major biographies: *Saint Genet* and *The Idiot of the Family*. As a social, psychological, and philosophical work, it is filled with surprises that will enlarge and alter our previous conceptions of existentialist thought.